CLEAN *Southern* CUISINE

WHERE SOUTHERN FOOD COMES CLEAN!

GLUTEN FREE * PALEO * CLEAN EATING

"Life's just too short to turn down champagne, eat mediocre food, or deal with unnecessary bullshit."

— AMANDA GIPSON NOWOSADZKI

Written by Amanda Gipson Nowosadzki

Photography and Food Styling by Amanda and Robert Nowosadzki

Foreword by Dr. Izabella Wentz

ISBN: 978-1-7349973-0-9

Oak + Iris Media

For information Contact:
www.cleansoutherncuisine.com
info@cleansoutherncuisine.com

Written by Amanda Gipson Nowosadzki
Photography and Food Styling by Amanda and Robert Nowosadzki
Foreword by Dr. Izabella Wentz - www.thyroidpharmacist.com
Design & Illustrations by Kate Ferry - kateferry33@mac.com

Disclaimer: The content within this book is for entertainment purposes only. The author is not a doctor or medical professional and the content of this book is not intended to replace the advice or direction of a medical professional. The author will not be held liable for any medical issues, loss, or damage caused or allegedly caused by any methods, recipes, or suggestions contained within this book. You should always consult a qualified medical professional prior to starting a new diet or lifestyle.

First Edition: June 2020

TABLE OF CONTENTS

ABOUT THIS BOOK

When you think of the most flavor-robust foods you've ever tasted, Louisiana, New Orleans, or "Cajun Country" might come to mind. If you ask around, many people's "best meal ever" was in the South and often in New Orleans. This book is firmly rooted in that culinary region.

While it seems that Southern food and "nutritious" or "healthy" don't intersect, it's my mission to challenge that. Southern food doesn't have to be horrible for you in order to be delicious, and the recipes on the following pages will prove it to you.

In addition to original recipes, I've taken quite a few delicacies that are traditional to the area and reformulated them to be more nutritious and free of common food irritants. BY NO MEANS does this mean they skimp on flavor! If you are a skeptic, just try the gumbo on page 61 or the pound cake on page 135.

Like many good Southern recipes, a lot of these begin with a story, or were passed down from a family member or close friend. It's my hope that you will gather around a table with those you hold dear and share these recipes in good company.

Cheers to your delicious journey to clean eating!

For more resources, information, shopping lists, and new recipes please visit my website:

www.cleansoutherncuisine.com

ABOUT THE AUTHOR

"Life's just too short to turn down champagne, eat mediocre food, or deal with unnecessary bullshit."

— AMANDA GIPSON NOWOSADZKI

Lucky for me I hail from one of the far reaches of the country.... Cajun Country or South Louisiana. My hometown of roughly 30,000 people – New Iberia, Louisiana – is a mecca for Cajun cuisine. The food is a pillar of the of the rich cultural heritage. Sublime yet humble food is not only commonplace but tradition. It's oozing with robust history, flavor, and personality. The connection between food and family is a tightly intertwined one and we'd rather do a lot of things than share mediocre food with our loved ones.

Let me take y'all back a bit. My culinary education began in my wonderful mother's kitchen. Yes, y'all… it was Louann's kitchen. The rest of us were welcomed in, but it was Mom that created the magic and passed down traditions to me and my two sisters. Even as a child I knew that we weren't wealthy, but were rich in the important ways…like love and really good food. I realized early on that my mom was an excellent cook, and I learned to create the region's cuisine at her hip.

My education and love for food continued to evolve while I worked in the catering and hospitality industry in New Orleans. Living in NOLA was a foodie's dream and simultaneously a regional culinary education. I dined almost daily at restaurants ranging from cozy "hole in the wall" to white tablecloth, fine dining establishments. I was then in my 20's and I'm fairly certain about 50% of my paycheck was spent on dining out! Needless to say, my love and knowledge of food continued to grow in one of the best food cities on the planet.

However, it wasn't until I moved out of state that I could fully appreciate what a special thing we have in our Louisiana cuisine. Now, let's get real here y'all. Most of the food stars of Louisiana and the South aren't exactly healthy. I decided to create the same flavorful food in a healthier manner. A manner that still honors the tradition of the region but packs more nutrition. It also needed to be suitable for those with celiac disease, other autoimmune conditions, those who want to lose weight, or those who simply seek to feel better and have better health.

Above all else, I didn't want these recipes to lack in flavor or authenticity as a result. I've made it my business to ensure that anyone tasting these recipes simply won't know they are "clean". To the consumer of these recipes it's just good Southern food. The silver lining is that it's so much more than that!

WHY EAT THIS WAY?

My first experience with "clean eating" was just before my thirtieth birthday. I decided to try the Paleo diet for a period of time. In truth, my reasoning was that I wanted to lose a couple of extra pounds that seemed to have crept on. I remember talking with my sister in law (see the foreword) who was already well versed in clean eating. She mentioned to me that I should write down any "symptoms or health issues" I was experiencing as most people see major improvements when they eliminate gluten, dairy, and other inflammatory foods from their diets. I remember thinking "symptoms?", "health issues?"... I felt puzzled as I thought, "but I don't have any of those".

Well low and behold, after two weeks on the paleo diet the painful tendinitis in my wrists was gone. After about a month, my ongoing digestive issues (IBS) had drastically improved. Were these the symptoms and health issues my sister in law was referring to? Yes, they were. However, I'd actually learned to live with them and accepted them as my "normal". Conventional medicine told me that unless I wanted to take pills these symptoms would be a part of my life from now on. It simply didn't occur to me that food could literally heal me from the inside out. Or furthermore, that food, (the wrong food in this case) was the primary cause of these issues in the first place!

This was undeniable proof in my own body and my perception of food began to change rapidly.

So you may be wondering, "what about the weight you wanted to lose"? In the first week I dropped 5 lbs. In the three following weeks I lost another 5 lbs, and it was as if inflammation was fleeing from my body. I never once before made a correlation between the food I ate and the inflammation that resulted. Sure, I knew that my stomach would ache or I'd have a digestive flare up if I ate something that "didn't agree with me". However, I never thought about the inflammation this was causing throughout my entire body - for example in my wrists.

The tendinitis in my wrists was irritated by simple activities, like typing or chopping, making it very limiting to experience this day in and day out. Forget working out or doing weight bearing activities! After trying numerous treatment avenues (chiropractors, orthopedic doctors, topical creams, physical therapy, stretches, exercises) I stumbled upon a solution I never suspected - food!

Perhaps you have similar issues. Perhaps for you it's a desire to lose weight, become more healthy, or a desire to overcome a health condition. Or maybe you just feel achy and bloated. If any of these apply to you or someone you care about read on.

DIETS, LIFESTYLES, AND GLUTEN

While you'll find an array of recipes within that target different diets or lifestyles, (Paleo, AIP, Ketogenic, etc) you'll note that none of them contain gluten. Gluten generally refers to the protein found in wheat, rye, and barley. It truly is the "glue" that holds things together. For most of us, it's also a major cause of systemic inflammation in our bodies.

As I previously mentioned, when I removed gluten from my diet my ongoing digestive issues (IBS) improved dramatically. Also, avoiding gluten was the only thing that finally made my persistent tendinitis pain go away.

Many people experience happy byproducts of eliminating gluten from their diets. Like me, you've likely learned to live with digestive issues, aches and pains, or inflammation. Perhaps you've grown so accustomed to these things that you just accept them as your own "normal". You'll be shocked at how much better you can feel every day when you no longer consume gluten.

WHAT TO AVOID

We are all different, and I recommend finding what works for you. Eliminating processed foods and gluten from your diet are a great place to start. What you do from there is up to you….what foods serve your body? What foods cause you inflamation and achiness? What foods do you occasionally want to enjoy? (See "Sweets and Treats" and "Biscuits and Breads" chapters!).

Here are the things I absolutely recommend avoiding:
Gluten, GMOs or Genetically Modified Organisms (corn and soy are the most prevalent), Processed Foods, Canola Oil, and High Fructose Corn Syrup.

READ THE LABELS!

When you make a commitment to eat clean, you'll be purchasing less and less processed foods. However, if you get into the simple habit of reading the ingredient lists on the packaged foods you do buy, you will become more aware of what is actually in your food. In turn, you'll have more control over your health and what you choose to put into your body. When you see ingredients like canola oil, soybean oil, soy, or high fructose corn syrup you'll know to steer clear of these items. Remember this tip: Extremely long ingredient lists, or ingredients you've never heard of and can't pronounce tend to be indicative of highly processed food.

*Learn more and get a complete list of foods and ingredients to avoid by visiting the resources section of my website. www.cleansoutherncuisine.com

ON TREATS AND GOODIES

In my opinion, it's not sustainable for most people to eliminate all sugars and treats from their lifestyles permanently. I absolutely recognize that eating extremely clean for a period of time (think Whole 30) is wonderful and extremely beneficial for some people with health conditions, or those looking to shed some pounds safely. It certainly helped me.

However, I do believe that if you have your health conditions in check you should be able to enjoy a sweet or treat from time to time. The recipes in my "Sweets and Treats" and "Biscuits and Breads" chapters are crafted to contain the highest levels of minerals and nutrients possible, while still tasting like a sweet, treat, biscuit, or bread. So, in moderation, these can be enjoyed.

Unfortunately, this is not carte blanche to eat as many cookies or bread as you want… sorry y'all. You are still consuming carbohydrates and sugar even if the ingredients are much cleaner, so you still want to do so reasonably. As is the case with all of my recipes, I've set out to create harmony between healthy ingredients and the traditional tastes and textures we are accustomed to.

WHAT TO EXPECT

When you fully eliminate processed foods and focus on real nutrient-dense foods, your palate will start to change. For example, if you dedicate yourself to eating this way for 3 - 4 weeks and then have a highly processed item you may notice it tastes far different than it did before… maybe way too sugary, too salty, or just fake. You likely won't get the same natural "lift" you do from eating clean whole foods.

It's best to be equipped with the knowledge that when you stop consuming refined sugar and processed foods, you will usually experience intense cravings for such items. Don't give up and retreat to your old sugar-laden or processed favorites! After 3 - 4 weeks of eating this way you will notice these cravings will really start to lessen, and it gets easier from there.

Pay attention to how you feel after eating different foods. Chances are if you slip up and have a highly processed or sugary item you won't feel very good afterwards. I'm not referring to guilt here, as I highly recommend avoiding this if you do slip up. None of us is perfect and guilt will do more harm than good. What I mean is actually physical sensations in your body, your mental clarity, etc. You may experience a sugar high then slump, you may feel like your thoughts are a bit cloudy, or your joints might feel achy the day afterward. Just pay attention to what your body is trying to tell you!

In addition to your palate changing, you may notice that you drop a few pounds, have less inflamation/pain in your body, and just generally feel better!

WHAT FOODS TO ENJOY!

Stock your refrigerator and pantry with foods that will enable you to feel better, look better, and achieve better health. Please visit the resources section of my website for a more complete list and for easy links to purchase these items.

REFRIGERATED ITEMS

ITEM	WHAT TO LOOK FOR	SOURCE/TRUSTED BRANDS
Eggs	Free Range and Organic. Large Brown are used in recipes unless otherwise noted.	Organic Valley Omega 3 Organic Free Range Eggs
Chicken and other Poultry	Free Range and Organic. Antibiotic Free.	Butcherbox.com or your grocer
Beef	Grass Fed and Organic. Antibiotic Free.	Butcherbox.com or your grocer
Bacon	Uncured, Nitrate Free, Antibiotic Free. No Sugar in ingredient list.	Applegate Farms
Deli Meats	Nitrate and Nitrite Free, Antibiotic Free	Applegate Farms
Mustard	No sugar	Annie's Organic Dijon or Yellow Mustard.
Mayonnaise	No canola or soybean oil	Sir Kensington's classic or organic mayonnaise. or better yet try the basic mayo recipe on pg 105!
Ketchup	No high fructose corn syrup or soybean oil.	Ketchups still contain sugar so use in moderation or try the Smoky Spanish Sauce on pg 95. Annie's Organic Ketchup
Coconut Aminos (soy sauce alternative)	Organic	Coconut Secret
Milk	Coconut Milk (canned) Nut milks (homeade are best as they don't contain gums and unnecessary sugar)	Native Forest Organic "Simple" coconut milk
Butter	Grass fed and organic if you can tolerate dairy.	Kerrygold
Dairy Cream and Milk	Organic and grass fed if you can tolerate dairy.	Organic Valley
Produce	Organic and Non GMO	Shop the organic section at a local grocery, go to a farmer's market when possible, or research CSAs in your area.

PANTRY ITEMS

ITEM	WHAT TO LOOK FOR	SOURCE/TRUSTED BRANDS
Canned Fish (Salmon, Tuna)	Wild Caught	Wild Planet, Trader Joes, or sometimes Costco.
Raw Nuts	Organic	Costco, Trader Joes, Amazon
Coconut Milk	The only ingredient should be coconut milk. Buy Organic when possible	Native Forest Simple
Coconut Oil	Organic, Cold Pressed, and Unrefined	Nutiva
Palm Shortening	Organic and Non Hydrogenated	Spectrum
Ghee	Grass Fed and Organic	Organic Valley or 14th and Heart
Avocado Oil	Cold Pressed	Chosen Foods
Olive Oil	Extra Virgin, should not say refined	Napa Valley Naturals
Apple Cider Vinegar	Organic With "the mother"	Bragg
Salt	Sea Salt	Redmond Real Sea Salt - Fine
Seasonings, Spices, Dried Herbs	Organic	Simply Organic
Almond Flour	Extra Fine or Super Fine, Blanched, Organic	Wellbee's Super Fine
Sorghum, Arrowroot, Tapioca, Potato Starch, Brown Rice Flour, Golden Flaxseed Meal		Bob's Red Mill brand is suitable for all of these flours and can be found in many major grocers
Flaxseed	Organic whole (golden or brown) flaxseeds. Whenever possible purchase whole flaxseeds and grind them yourself just before using. This way you reap all of the nutritional benefits.	Bob's Red Mill brand
Raw Cacao	Organic, from unroasted cacao beans	Navitas organics
Cassava	Organic, Raw	Otto's Naturals
Coconut Sugar	Organic, Raw	Mudhavva, Navitas, Bob's Red Mill
Agave Nectar	Organic	Wholesome Brand
Maple Syrup	Organic	Coomb's Family Farms

PANTRY ITEMS *(continued)*

ITEM	WHAT TO LOOK FOR	SOURCE/TRUSTED BRANDS
Chia Seeds		Navitas organics
Nut butters	Organic Raw when possible (higher nutrient content)	Once Again brand
Dried Fruit	No sugar added, unsulfured.	Now Foods
Coconut Water	100% coconut water (only ingredient)	Zico, Taste Nirvana, or Harmless Harvest
Collagen Peptides		Vital Proteins

HELPFUL KITCHEN TOOLS

ITEM	WHAT TO LOOK FOR
High Powered Blender	If there is one item I recommend above all else it's a high powered blender (like Vitamix). I know these blenders are not cheap but they will quickly become a workhorse in your kitchen. They also enable you to convert whole foods into delicious recipes with little effort - think nut butters, juices, etc.
Cast Iron Skillet/Pan	What Southern kitchen doesn't have a good cast iron skillet?! Plus there are no questionable non-stick coatings to be concerned with.
Mandoline	You'll never make scalloped potatoes without this again.
Microplane	For grating citrusy goodness into baked goods, salads, etc.
Whisk	Necessary for many of the recipes in this book.
Rolling Pin	You'll need one of these for the sesame crackers, pie crusts, etc.
Food Processor	I like to make large batches of recipes which sometimes requires a lot of vegetables or chopping. A food processor will really make your life easier.
Spiralizer	You can make your own veggie noodles to lighten up classic dishes like spaghetti.

ASTERISKS IN THE RECIPE TAGS
Ex: *VEGAN* / PALEO / AIP / KETOGENIC / NUT FREE / GLUTEN FREE
The asterisk next to "vegan" tells you that a simple substitution (notated in the recipe) will make it vegan.

ON BAKING
You always want to sift, or at least whisk, your ingredients prior to measuring. While traditional wheat flours can be more forgiving, you will find that using too much gluten free flour typically results in a gummy baked good. So if you used to skimp by without sifting or whisking (like me) these extra steps will really reward you when working with alternative flours.

DEDICATION

This book is dedicated to my angels who continue to inspire and guide me today.

Bernice B Gipson (Granny)
*A pioneer female business owner in the 50s and a Southern lady
who was unafraid to speak her mind. Much of her china is featured
throughout the book and I'm so grateful to be named after her.*

Mary Ingrid Nelson Jones
*A grand lady, teacher, and poet. Her front porch has always been
a special place and will always remain so. I've always loved spending time there
and enjoyed doing so during a photo shoot for this book.*

David Cole
*A great mentor to me and a man who sought to find or create humor
and have fun every single day. You taught us to tap into our inner child
and not take life so seriously…It's a gift I still carry with me.*

Mike Vidallier
*An unintentionally cool guy and an incredible father and husband.
Thank you for reminding us how to live joyfully and laugh
at the little everyday stuff of life.*

ON LIVING AND DINING IN NEW ORLEANS

Having a meal in New Orleans is more than just consuming food. It's a journey through flavor in which you can taste the passion and pride that guided the hands of the chef, the local farmer, and the tight-knit community that supports them.

Your meal is served and upon first bites you exchange a knowing smile with the next table or patron as you both feel, for a moment, that you're a part of an exclusive private club that only those who are dining beside you or have been there before you can truly understand.

This experience knows no boundaries. Make no mistake that this can happen anywhere. From the convivial wallpapered rooms of Commander's Palace to the worn and tattered bar room at Parasol's, as the juices from a roast beef Po'boy run down your hands. You'll be thinking about what you tasted and what you felt a part of for weeks to come....

In those weeks you'll likely require at least one costume and encounter at least one parade. In New Orleans we don't just have a costume box. We have elaborate costume wardrobes and may donn any of them on any old day of the week. It's also hard to go a week without stumbling upon a parade of some sort. It may be a "foot" parade or something more elaborate but you don't need a reason or an excuse for festivities in NOLA. It takes all kinds.

ON GROWING UP IN SOUTH LOUISIANA'S "CAJUN COUNTRY"

The Romero brothers played the accordion and triangle under the Evangeline Oak in St. Martinville, LA for years. For those of us old enough to remember them we witnessed something I love most about that part of the world. The humbleness of the local people and their recognition of and appreciation for simple pleasures. These pleasures may be lost on many others (who might be put off by the mosquitoes or extreme humidity) but the people of this region are really good at creating their own happiness. They realize that it's the simple things that are not to be scoffed at. Catching or trapping your own seafood dinner, a glass of cold ice tea (or beer!) on your screened porch, getting together with family for a boil or big home cooked meal, or exploring our particular brand of nature - swamps, bayous, and inlets.

Growing up I spent a fair amount of time canoeing in the local bayous. I will never forget the first time I met an alligator while in a canoe. I must have been 8 or 9 and the low sides of a canoe can make you feel pretty vulnerable! That said I was taught to remain calm around wildlife. So I held my breath and slipped quietly past it. There is something incredible about these prehistoric-like creatures living right in our midst that contributes to the overall experience. Times like these taught me from an early age to respect our very special wildlife, flora, and fauna in the swamps and inlets of South Louisiana. I'm eternally grateful that all of this was the backdrop for my youth.

Foreword

By Dr. Izabella Wentz

As a pharmacist who has seen that food can be just as powerful of a medicine as modern pharmaceuticals, I am so excited about Clean Southern Cuisine! As a result of my own health journey with the chronic autoimmune condition Hashimoto's hypothyroidism, I have dedicated my professional career to helping people take back their health through lifestyle change. The message that genes are not our destiny and that through the choices we make in our daily lives we hold the power to recover our own health is a truth I have seen time and time again, not just in the lives of my clients, but also in my own life.

You may think that disease is in your genes and that being sick is "your destiny", " a result of getting older" or "just a normal occurrence", and that the only answer to health struggles is to take a prescription to "manage" your symptoms.

In my early days as a pharmacist, I too thought this way. After all, I had extensive training in pharmacology! Therefore, I was constantly recommending medications. Acid reflux? Take acid suppressing medications! Irritable bowel syndrome? Take some anti-diarrheal pills! Pain? Pain medications to the rescue. Depression? Antidepressants! Every ill had a pill, but yet people weren't really getting better. The woman with acid reflux and irritable bowel syndrome eventually started coming in to get medications to treat an underactive thyroid, migraines and insomnia. The man with pain became addicted to painkillers. The woman with depression continued to struggle with depression, and eventually her weight and libido suffered as well.

Don't get me wrong, I'm very passionate about proper use of medications and am a big believer that medications save lives, but medications are not the be all end all to health, especially when it comes to the chronic health conditions that have become all too common in modern America.

In fact, in some cases, medications can even make us sicker. Sometimes it's because they act as bandaids suppressing the real causes of our illness, and in other cases, through directly causing disease by ways of nutrient deficiencies. The longer I worked as a pharmacist, the more I began to see that instead of medications being the cure, often times, medications would create new symptoms, that required even more medications to manage, that in turn then created more disease!

But what if I told you that symptoms like acid reflux, irritable bowel syndrome, migraines, pain and depression all have a common root cause? And what if I told you that there was a safer, more proactive and effective approach, that would help you eliminate your symptoms, as well as in some cases, prevent, reduce or eliminate your need for medications.

This brings me to the food we eat….

Time and time again I have seen symptoms like joint pain, fatigue, headaches, digestive issues and many others disappear, just through changing our diets!

I have seen that food as medicine (or food pharmacology, as I like to call it) can create profound transformations in a person's health. Food has the power to nourish us, balance our stress hormones, improve our digestion and support our detoxification pathways, yet our standard Western diet is often lacking the highly nourishing foods that support health. Instead, the foods present in the Western diet are causing inflammation, digestive distress and blood sugar imbalances.

Every system is perfectly designed to produce the results it produces. If we continue to eat inflammatory foods, we will continue to be inflamed. If we continue to eat foods that are causing blood sugar imbalances, we will continue to have an epidemic of diabetes. In order to get our health back, we must break free from the conventional, and we have to take charge of our own healing destiny. I have seen people feel better with proper nutrition than with medications. Every time we eat a meal, we have a choice to support or diminish the body's inner healing capabilities.

With time, I realized that nutrition is the cornerstone of our health. Nowadays, I don't just recommend food before medicine, I recommend food as medicine. Let this guide be the start of your healing journey!

While some people may have an understanding that diet may help, there is also a natural hesitation in changing one's diet. I know many people are afraid that eating a clean diet may mean boiled chicken and steamed vegetables for breakfast, lunch and dinner. Fear not! Amanda's passion for culinary excellence stems from her Southern roots with a big influence from New Orleans, "Cajun Country", and the flavor-robust foods of those culinary regions.

Amanda is one of those rare people who can turn even the simplest meal into a delicious celebration. She has been where you are and has come out on the other side of healing. She radiates warmth, kindness and southern hospitality. After all, if you're going to change your diet, you may as well eat delicious food and have fun in the process, right?

Amanda and I met in 2012 when she and my brother Robert first started dating, but even before we officially met, I heard endless praise of her cooking skills. In addition to being beautiful, kind and compassionate, my brother raved about her cooking! I'm always thanking my brother for getting me a brilliant, kind and talented new sister (in love)!

I am always inspired by Amanda....her kindness, desire to help others, creativity and brilliance really shine in the pages of this book. I'm proud to say that after tasting some of her mouth-watering recipes I insisted that she take the time to create this cookbook to share her delicious cuisine with the world.

I've had the pleasure of experiencing Amanda's cooking time and time again, from weekday get togethers, to potlucks and holiday parties, Amanda's dishes are always a hit with every guest. I've been privy to enjoy Bananas Foster Smoothie and her Fluffy Paleo Waffles on a weekend brunch, then the Pecan Crusted Okra Fries, Pastalaya, Crab Cakes and Crawfish Pie during a fun dinner. Amanda's Belle of the Ball Biscuits (which stole the show at a recent Thanksgiving celebration), Amaretto Pound Cake, Orange Sponge Cake, and Mini Blueberry Scones at family birthday parties.

In Clean Southern Cuisine, Amanda takes you on a culinary journey that will awaken your body's healing capabilities. Whether you've been an avid dieter for some time, or new to the world of nutrition, the recipes in this book will help you reduce the inflammation in your body, increase your intake of healing nutrients and balance your blood sugar. I call these effects the fundamentals of healing and Amanda's recipes will help every single person who wants to optimize their own body's function with nutrition.

Doing just these fundamentals will help you feel significantly better, and may even reverse lifelong symptoms like blood sugar imbalances, mood swings, panic attacks, breakouts, menstrual cramps, digestive issues and joint pains, that you may have thought were "just a part of your genetic makeup", "a result of getting older" or "just a normal occurrence".

Because they're so delicious-Amanda's recipes can also be served to the whole family, in fact they've been huge hits at all of our family's gatherings! Your loved ones will love the foods you feed them, and chances are, they won't even realize that they're eating "healthy" food!

In some cases, you may also notice that your friends and family members will want to adopt this style of eating and you will begin to see that they too, will feel healthier and more balanced as a result.

I am so grateful for Amanda for sharing her passion for delicious food and vibrant health to create this beautiful guide. I know that utilizing the recipes in this book will bring you many mouthwatering meals, transformative healing, and endless praise from loved ones lucky enough to taste your cooking.

To your health!

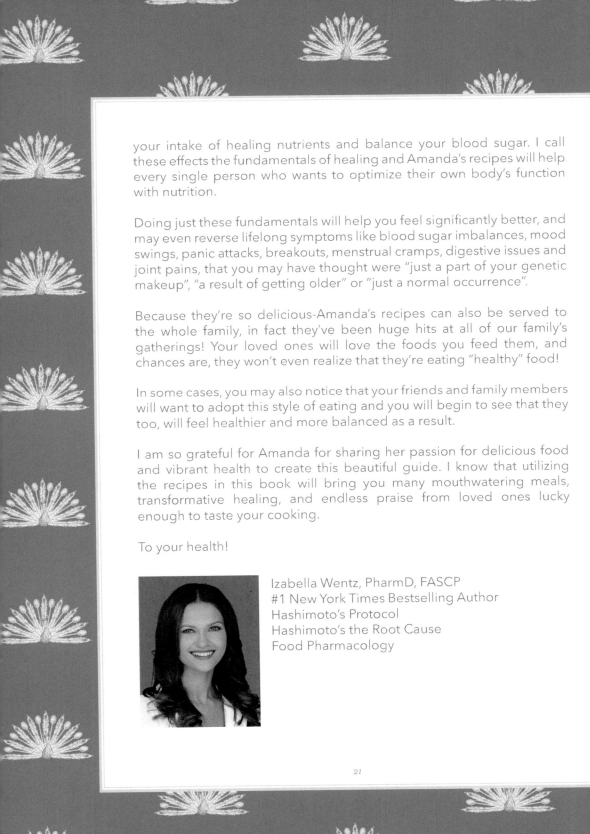

Izabella Wentz, PharmD, FASCP
#1 New York Times Bestselling Author
Hashimoto's Protocol
Hashimoto's the Root Cause
Food Pharmacology

Breakfast & Brunch

cleansoutherncuisine.com

BANANAS FOSTER SMOOTHIE

Does anyone else like having dessert for breakfast? This iconic New Orleans dessert gets a makeover for your blender. There may not be a dramatic tableside preparation involving flambé or rum but you won't miss either when you get to have this treat for breakfast! Be sure to use unsulfured blackstrap molasses. It contains nutrients and minerals you won't get otherwise!

YIELD:
1 serving (2 cups)

INGREDIENTS:

1 c non-dairy milk of choice

1 frozen banana

1 serving vanilla protein powder of choice

2 t unsulfured blackstrap molasses

1/8 t cinnamon

seeds from one vanilla bean, optional

PROCESS:
Place all ingredients in blender

Blend until fully combined and pour into glass

Top fresh banana slices, if desired, and enjoy!

*Notes: Coconut, cashew, or almond milk will work well with this recipe. *To make this recipe keto-friendly, substitute yacon syrup for the molasses.*

About this Recipe
VEGAN / PALEO / DAIRY FREE / EGG FREE / AIP / KETOGENIC / VEGETARIAN / GLUTEN FREE*

DRINKABLE BERRY YOGURT

For those who can't tolerate dairy this yogurt is a welcome alternative. It's an extremely hands-off recipe and a great grab-and-go option for busy mornings. Blending in tasteless collagen peptides effortlessly increases the protein content. When picking a probiotic capsule, look for at least 1 billion CFU or 250 mg of the active ingredient. Saccharomyces Boulardii works well in this recipe.

YIELD:

2 ¼ c (2 servings)

INGREDIENTS:

1 can full fat coconut milk (13.5 oz)

2 capsules probiotics

1 c berries of choice

collagen peptides or protein powder of choice, optional.

PROCESS:

Pour coconut milk into a glass container.

Sprinkle contents of two probiotic capsules over liquid and stir well to combine.

Place in oven overnight with light on, no heat.

In the morning blend yogurt with frozen berries of your choosing until smooth. This may be done with a standard blender or an immersion blender.

Refrigerate and enjoy.

Notes: Use frozen berries if you want your yogurt to be cold immediately.

About this Recipe

VEGAN / PALEO / DAIRY FREE / EGG FREE / AIP / KETOGENIC / NUT FREE / VEGETARIAN / GLUTEN FREE

PUMPKIN PIE SMOOTHIE

Most of the things we associate with autumn are warm and inviting. This smoothie is no exception with it's pumpkin pie spice. Pumpkin is vitamin-rich and contains a lot of dietary fiber which will help you to feel full for longer. All of this accomplished with your first meal of the day and with very little effort!

YIELD:
2 cups

INGREDIENTS:
1/2 c canned or cooked pumpkin

1/2 c full fat coconut milk

1 t pumpkin pie spice

vanilla protein powder
(equivalent to 20 g protein)

1 c fresh baby spinach, optional

1/2 c ice

PROCESS:
Blend all ingredients together until smooth.

Top with toasted pumpkin seeds if desired.

Notes: If you choose to add spinach or other fresh greens you'll get even more vitamins and minerals and your smoothie will be green. The color can be a lot of fun for kids.

About this Recipe
VEGAN / PALEO / DAIRY FREE / EGG FREE / KETOGENIC / NUT FREE / VEGETARIAN / GLUTEN FREE

CHOCOLATE PUDDING

Chocolate pudding has always been a favorite of mine...but the store–bought variety is packed with not so desirable ingredients. This pudding is thickened with chia seeds. In addition to powerful antioxidants and fiber, chia seeds are a great source of protein. Traditional chia seed puddings use whole seeds and take lots of time to thicken. Grinding the seeds in your blender makes for an instant smooth and creamy texture and requires no waiting time.

YIELD:
2 1/2 cups (2 servings)

INGREDIENTS:
1 can light coconut milk (13.5 oz)

1/2 c black chia seeds

3 T raw cacao powder

1/2 t vanilla

1T agave nectar

collagen peptides or protein powder of choice
(equivalent of 30g protein)

PROCESS:
Place all ingredients in high-powered blender.

Blend, quickly increasing speed to high, for about a minute or until the mixture thickens significantly.

Refrigerate and Enjoy!

*Notes: If you'd like to consume this immediately, pre-refrigerate your coconut milk so your pudding will be cold. With added collagen peptides or protein this pudding is 27g of protein per serving! *To make this recipe keto-friendly, substitute yacon syrup for the agave.*

About this Recipe
VEGAN / PALEO / DAIRY FREE / EGG FREE / AIP / KETOGENIC / NUT FREE / VEGETARIAN / GLUTEN FREE*

BANANA WALNUT BREAKFAST COOKIES

These cookies make a great portable breakfast but are quite delicious any time of day! Think banana bread in a cookie format. They are low-carbohydrate and will give you lots of energy due to the protein and fat content. As an added bonus, this recipe comes together in a snap and uses only one bowl!

YIELD:

2 dozen

INGREDIENTS:

3 T golden flaxseed meal

6 T water

3 bananas

1/4 c coconut oil, melted

2 T agave

1 t vanilla extract

1 t baking soda

1/4 t cinnamon

1/2 t salt

3/4 c almond flour

3/4 c arrowroot flour

2 T coconut flour

1 c walnuts, chopped and lightly toasted

PROCESS:

In a medium mixing bowl combine flaxseed meal and water. Allow to sit for 3 minutes before adding bananas and mashing.

Add coconut oil, agave and vanilla. Stir to combine.

Stir in baking soda, cinnamon, and salt.

Stir in almond flour, arrowroot flour, and coconut flour until there are no clumps.

Stir in walnuts.

Cover and refrigerate dough for 30 minutes. While dough is setting, preheat oven to 350 degrees F.

Scoop rounded tablespoons of dough onto parchment lined baking sheet.

Bake for 17 - 20 minutes, or until light brown.

Notes: Flax seeds must be ground or bought as flaxseed meal (already ground).

About this Recipe
VEGAN / PALEO / DAIRY FREE / EGG FREE / VEGETARIAN / GLUTEN FREE

BACON SHALLOT AND PEA QUICHE

Quiche is such a comfort food. It's like having a pie for breakfast! A traditional quiche actually uses quite a bit of cream and the cream to egg ratio makes for its silken custard–like texture. This quiche doesn't use any cream so it's almost like a frittata with a crust, however, you won't get any complaints!

YIELD:

1 quiche

INGREDIENTS:

1 pre-baked pie crust
(see pages X and X)

1 package bacon,
chopped into 1/2 pieces

2 shallots, about 1/2 c, minced

3/4 c frozen or fresh sweet peas

10 large eggs

1 T water

1 c grated cheese, optional

1 T dill

1 t thyme

3/4 t salt

1/2 t pepper

PROCESS:

Prick the pie crust several times with a fork and pre-bake it (no filling) for 15 minutes at 350 degrees.

Meanwhile, cook chopped bacon in a skillet over medium heat until done. Add in shallots and peas and cook for an additional 5 minutes.

In a mixing bowl beat eggs, water, and seasoning.

Once bacon mixture has cooled add it into the eggs and stir.

Pour egg mixture into pre-baked pie crust. Bake for 35 - 45 minutes at 350 degrees.

Notes: Pre-baking the pie crust will keep it from getting soggy. Bake quiche until eggs are set with just a bit of wobble in the middle.

About this Recipe
PALEO / DAIRY FREE / COCONUT FREE / NUT FREE / VEGETARIAN / GLUTEN FREE

TOMATO AND ONION FRITTATA

Frittatas are so much easier than they seem. They come together quickly and puff up in the oven making for an elegant presentation. It's a great option to feed a crowd or to simply have leftovers throughout the week.

YIELD:
6 - 8 servings

INGREDIENTS:
1 T avocado oil or olive oil

1 c onion, chopped small

10 eggs

2 T water

3/4 t + ¼ t salt

1/2 t black pepper

1/4 t white pepper

2 T green onions

3 - 5 thin slices of tomato

PROCESS:
In a 10" skillet, saute onions over medium high heat until translucent, about 7 - 9 minutes. Add 1/4 t salt.

Meanwhile, in a separate bowl, beat eggs with 2 T water, seasonings, and green onions.

Lower heat to medium low and pour egg mixture into skillet.

Stir occasionally until the bottom of the frittata is set.

Transfer skillet to top rack in oven and broil for 3 minutes.

Remove from oven and top with tomato slices

Return to oven to broil for another 3 minutes, monitoring carefully so eggs become just brown, not burnt.

Slice and enjoy!

Notes: This frittata reheats well. Make it over the weekend and enjoy it throughout the week.

About this Recipe
PALEO / DAIRY FREE / KETOGENIC / COCONUT FREE / NUT FREE / VEGETARIAN / GLUTEN FREE

FLUFFY PALEO WAFFLES

Waffles generally elicit smiles all around. These waffles are no exceptions. Plus they are no muss, no fuss. You can mix them right in the blender and pour directly from your blender container into your waffle iron. Pair these waffles with my strawberry collagen topping (visit website for recipe) for 13 g of protein per serving!

YIELD:
4 standard round waffles

INGREDIENTS:
3 Eggs

1 c full fat coconut milk

1/4 c club soda or water

1 T agave

1/2 t vanilla

1 3/4 t cream of tartar

3/4 t baking soda

pinch salt

1 c cassava flour

PROCESS:
Dump all ingredients into blender and blend until smooth.

Use standard size round waffle iron per manufacturer's instructions.

Notes: Coconut allergy? Sub 2/3 c nut milk like cashew or almond + 1/4 c avocado oil in place of the coconut milk.

About this Recipe
PALEO / DAIRY FREE / NUT FREE / VEGETARIAN / GLUTEN FREE

Appetizers & Snacks

TOASTED SESAME CRACKERS

These tasty crackers are high in protein and oh so satisfying! Unlike store-bought gluten free crackers they contain no soy, unnecessary sugar, or preservatives. These are a great sidekick to a cured meats platter but there is no end to the possibilities.

YIELD:

About 40 crackers

INGREDIENTS:

1/4 c toasted organic brown sesame seeds

1 cup blanched fine almond flour

2 T golden flaxseed meal

2 T coconut flour

1 t pink himalayan sea salt

2 flax eggs (2T of golden flax meal and 6T of water)

1 t raw organic honey

2 T palm shortening, melted

PROCESS:

Preheat oven to 300 degrees F.

Toast sesame seeds in a skillet with no oil, about 10-12 minutes, over a medium low heat. Give the skillet a shake every 2 minutes or so to evenly toast.

Whisk together the first five ingredients in a medium mixing bowl.

Make 2 flax eggs by combining 2 T golden flaxseed meal and 6T water. Set aside for 5 minutes.

Melt honey and shortening in a small mixing bowl. Add flax eggs and stir well to combine.

Pour liquid into dry ingredients and stir vigorously until a dough is formed.

On parchment paper, roll out dough to 1/8 inch thickness. Use arrowroot powder to flour surface and rolling pin.

Use a 2" cookie cutter for round crackers or use a knife or pizza wheel to make square crackers about 2"X 2". Prick each cracker twice with a fork.

Carefully transfer crackers to a parchment lined cookie sheet.

Bake for 10 minutes. Remove from oven and carefully flip crackers. Bake for 10 more minutes, or until golden in color.

Cool and Enjoy!

Notes: Cover loosely and store for up to 2 days.

About this Recipe
VEGAN / PALEO / DAIRY FREE / EGG FREE / VEGETARIAN / GLUTEN FREE

DEVILED EGGS – TWO WAYS

Deviled eggs can certainly be deemed a Southern classic. These two varieties step up the flavor profile. They will be a hit at any social gathering or provide a great healthy snack at home.

YIELD:
12 deviled egg halves

INGREDIENTS:
6 whole eggs, hard boiled

For Pimento Deviled Eggs:
4 oz jar of pimentos , well drained
4T mayo
1/4 t salt
1 t dijon mustard
1/4 t paprika
pinch of cayenne
chives, for garnish

For Guacamole Bacon Deviled Eggs:
1/2 of an avocado
3 T mayo
1/2 t salt
1/4 t white pepper
1 t lime juice
bacon, for garnish
cilantro leaves, for garnish

PROCESS:
Hard boil and peel eggs.

Slice eggs in half, placing the yolks in a small bowl.

Mash egg yolks with a fork.

Add all other ingredients to the bowl and combine with a fork until smooth and creamy.

Spoon mixture back into the egg halves and garnish as desired.

Notes: Boiled eggs cooked in a pressure cooker like an Instant Pot peel effortlessly.

• *PHOTO ON PAGE 38-39*

About this Recipe
PALEO / DAIRY FREE / KETOGENIC / COCONUT FREE / NUT FREE / VEGETARIAN / GLUTEN FREE

PECAN CRUSTED OKRA FRIES

These okra "fries" employ a savory pecan "breading" in place of the traditional corn meal. Blanching the okra improves its texture and reduces slime while baking (rather than frying) makes for easy kitchen clean up and a lighter preparation. If possible, use a wire cooling rack on your baking sheet, to elevate the okra and allow for more crisping of the breading mixture.

YIELD:

4 servings

INGREDIENTS:

1 lb okra, whole

2 eggs

2 t water

1/2 c pecans

1/4 c white sesame seeds

1/4 c golden flaxseed meal

1 t salt, divided

1 t paprika

1/2 t garlic

1/4 t chili powder

1/8 t of cayenne

PROCESS:

In your processor or blender grind pecans with sesame seeds, flaxseed meal, ½ salt, and seasonings to make "breading". Put this in a shallow bowl and set it aside.

Wash and dry whole okra.

Blanch the okra by dropping them into boiling water, and then immediately plunging them into ice water to stop cooking. (Blanch smaller okra for 3 minutes and larger okra for 4 minutes.) Remove from ice water and pat dry with a towel.

Whisk together egg, water, and ½ t salt in a mixing bowl to make an eggwash. Add okra to the bowl and toss until each piece is coated in the eggwash.

Holding okra by the top, roll each piece in the breading mixture until lightly coated. Place directly onto the wire rack set in a baking sheet. Repeat until all are coated.

Bake at 375 for 15 minutes, gently flip, and bake for another 10 minutes, or until the coating is crisp and the inside is tender.

Notes: Great with Smoky Spanish Sauce (pg. 95)

About this Recipe
PALEO / DAIRY FREE / KETOGENIC / COCONUT FREE / VEGETARIAN / GLUTEN FREE

SHRIMP AND CRAB HUSHPUPPIES

For me, hushpuppies conjure up images of informal seafood restaurants in the South, with unpretentious red and white checkered plastic table coverings and heavenly food. These hushpuppies skip the genetically modified cornmeal and canola oil but could easily pass for their casual seafood eatery counterparts.

YIELD:
6 - 8 servings (about 3 dozen)

INGREDIENTS:
1 c cornmeal, non GMO
1/3 c arrowroot flour
1 1/2 t baking powder
1/2 t salt
1 1/2 t garlic powder
1 t paprika
1/2 t chili powder
1/4 t cayenne

1/2 c unflavored non dairy milk, like macadamia, almond, or cashew
2 t lemon juice
1 T fish sauce

1/3 c green onions, chopped
1/2 c sweet onion, grated
1/2 c shrimp, chopped small or ground
1/2 c claw crabmeat

avocado oil or palm shortening, for frying

PROCESS:
Whisk dry ingredients together in a medium sized bowl.

Combine wet ingredients in a small bowl and add to dry.

Stir in green onions, sweet onions, shrimp, and crabmeat.

Preheat oil in a skillet or fryer per manufacturer instructions.

Using a small metal cookie scoop, drop hushpuppies gently into hot oil. They should be about a tablespoon.

Cook for about 4 minutes on medium high heat.

Transfer to paper towel lined plate to absorb excess oil and sprinkle with additional salt if desired.

Enjoy!

Notes: Be sure your cornmeal package has a non-GMO label. A small cookie/ice cream scoop will produce more rounded hushpuppies that will turn themselves as they fry - no flipping required. Red Boat brand fish sauce is available on Amazon. My favorite dipping sauce for these is remoulade (pg 91).

About this Recipe
DAIRY FREE / COCONUT FREE / GLUTEN FREE

ASIAN CAJUN PECANS

These are not your average pecans! The toasted sesame oil gives them a distinct Asian flare while the cayenne pepper and other spices draw out the Cajun influence. These become delightfully crisp in the oven and have a really pleasing crunch.

YIELD:

1 c pecans

INGREDIENTS:

1 c pecans

1 T maple syrup

1 T toasted sesame oil

1 1/2 T white or brown sesame seeds

3/4 t salt

1/2 t paprika

1/8 t chili powder

1/8 t garlic powder

1/8 t cayenne

PROCESS:

Preheat oven to 300 degrees F.

In a small glass bowl, mix together all ingredients except for the pecans.

Stir well to combine.

Add in pecans and stir until they are evenly coated.

Spread pecans onto a parchment lined baking sheet.

Bake for 10 minutes, flip, and then bake for another 10 minutes.

Remove from oven to cool.

Notes: The coating on these pecans will become crisp and is best enjoyed once they have cooled.

About this Recipe
VEGAN / PALEO / DAIRY FREE / EGG FREE / COCONUT FREE / VEGETARIAN / GLUTEN FREE

SHRIMP REMOULADE

A perfect appetizer, snack, brunch, lunch, or dinner item… shrimp remoulade is a classic New Orleans dish. It's tangy, zesty, and rich all at once. It's perfection on a plate served the traditional way – over greens – but it has quite a few applications.

YIELD:

3 - 4 servings

INGREDIENTS:

1/2 c remoulade sauce
(pg 91)

3 T celery

1 T green onion

1 T parsley

1 lb shrimp, peeled and cooked

PROCESS:

Combine remoulade sauce with finely chopped celery, green onion, and parsley.

Toss with shrimp and enjoy!

Notes: Shrimp remoulade can be served over greens or turned into a variety of appetizers. Try it on my Toasted Sesame Crackers (pg. 41)

About this Recipe
PALEO / DAIRY FREE / KETOGENIC / COCONUT FREE / NUT FREE / GLUTEN FREE

HAZELNUT CHOCOLATE BUTTER

This is the superfood version of chocolate hazelnut spreads many of us have come to love. With magnesium and antioxidants from the raw cacao and calcium and vitamin B from the hazelnuts you can't go wrong.

YIELD:

2 cups

INGREDIENTS:

2 T coconut oil

2 T raw agave nectar

3 T water

2 t vanilla

1/8 t salt

2 T raw cacao powder

2 c raw hazelnuts, whole

PROCESS:
Place all ingredients in your high-powered blender in the order listed.

Start blender and quickly increase speed while using the tamper to press ingredients down into the blades.

Blend until just smooth, taking care not to overheat blender motor.

*Notes: You will need a high-powered blender, like a Vitamix, for this recipe to work. A regular blender motor can not handle grinding nuts.
To make this recipe keto-friendly, omit the agave or substitute yacon syrup in its place.

About this Recipe
VEGAN / PALEO / DAIRY FREE / EGG FREE / KETOGENIC / VEGETARIAN / GLUTEN FREE*

CRAB DIABLA DIP

This savory and aromatic crab dip is irresistible. It's richness is perfectly balanced by spice making it a dip no one will soon forget. Try it with raw veggie sticks or plantain chips for a little crunch.

YIELD:

2 cups

INGREDIENTS:

1 lb crab meat
(lump is preferred)

1 c mayo

2 t lemon juice

1 c grated cheese of your
choice, optional*

2 t whole grain mustard

4 T green onions, chopped

4 T parsley, chopped

1/2 t garlic powder

1/2 t salt

1/4 t cayenne

1 t - 2 t hot sauce, or to your liking

PROCESS:
Preheat oven to 350 degrees F.

In a small mixing bowl combine all ingredients with the exception of the crabmeat. Stir until well combined.

Gently flake the crabmeat into the mixture and stir very briefly, just until coated.

Transfer to an oven safe dish and bake for 30 minutes.

Broil for an additional 5 minutes to brown top. Garnish with additional green onions and parsley before enjoying.

Notes: Turn up the heat with more cayenne and hot sauce! For a dip with some punch try a cheese with bold flavor - like parmesan.

About this Recipe
PALEO / DAIRY FREE / COCONUT FREE/ NUT FREE / GLUTEN FREE*

One Pot Meals & Soups

cleansoutherncuisine.com

SHRIMP SKILLET WITH KALE AND BLISTERED TOMATOES

Lazy lunch or dinner anyone? This flavor-packed one skillet meal is zesty and quick to throw together.

YIELD:

4 servings

INGREDIENTS:

2 lbs shrimp

2 cups cherry tomatoes, whole

2 bunches kale,
washed and chopped

2 T+ 1 T olive oil

2 t smoked paprika

1 teaspoon salt

1 t lemon juice, optional

MARINADE:

2 garlic cloves, chopped

2 t salt

2 t paprika

1/2 t Cayenne

2 T freshly squeezed lemon juice

4 T olive oil

PROCESS:

In a medium bowl make marinade. Mash garlic and salt together first then add all other marinade ingredients and stir.

Add shrimp and stir to coat.

Refrigerate for 30 minutes - overnight.

Using a large skillet, cook shrimp and any remaining marinade over medium heat until pink and opaque.

Transfer to a plate once cooked. Do not scrape or wipe the skillet. Add 1 T oil to the same skillet. Blister tomatoes over a medium heat, shuffling skillet every minute to turn tomatoes, about 8 - 10 minutes. Use caution as whole tomatoes will sometimes pop.

Add 2 T oil and kale to the skillet. Toss to coat kale in oil.

Add seasonings and allow kale to sautee/wither (about 5 minutes)

Add shrimp back to skillet and toss.

Add optional fresh lemon juice and enjoy!

About this Recipe
PALEO / DAIRY FREE / EGG FREE / KETOGENIC / COCONUT FREE/ NUT FREE / GLUTEN FREE

SPICY BISON CHILI

My dad has always appreciated a good hearty meal and he loves spice more than most. He grows several varieties of chilis in a special pepper garden and dries them to make his own seasoning. While this one pot meal won't be quite spicy enough for my Dad, I know he'll have his own custom pepper blend on hand to "doctor it up" a bit. For the rest of us, the chipotle powder imparts just the right amount of smokiness and heat to this chili. This one's for you Dad.

YIELD:
8 - 10 servings (without beans)

INGREDIENTS:
1 T olive oil
2 cups yellow onion
4 carrots
1 large green bell pepper
1/2 t salt
1/2 head cauliflower
1 zucchini
1 yellow squash
2 cloves of garlic, minced
2 lbs ground bison
2 c beef broth
2 T apple cider vinegar
4 T organic tomato paste
2 16 oz cans of organic beans
of your choice, optional

CHILI SEASONING BLEND:
2 1/2 t salt
1 t black pepper
1/2 t white pepper
2 T chili powder
1 1/2 t chipotle chile powder
1 1/2 t cumin
1 1/2 t paprika
1 1/2 t garlic powder
1 1/2 t dried oregano
1/2 t coriander

PROCESS:
Finely chop all vegetables in a food processor or by hand.

Using a large stock pot or soup pot, warm 1 T oil over a medium heat.

Add onions, carrots, bell peppers, and 1/2 t salt. Saute for 10 minutes, or until soft.

Next add cauliflower, zucchini, squash, and garlic. Saute for another 3 minutes, until garlic is fragrant.

Add ground bison and brown. Once meat has browned, add broth, chili seasoning blend, tomato paste, and vinegar.

Simmer over medium-low heat for 25 minutes, stirring occasionally.

Stir in optional beans and let simmer for another 10 minutes.

About this Recipe
PALEO / DAIRY FREE / EGG FREE / KETOGENIC / COCONUT FREE / NUT FREE / GLUTEN FREE*

CHICKEN AND ANDOUILLE GUMBO

Gumbo…. The iconic "everything but the kitchen sink" meal of Louisiana. Likely the most popularized and widely recognized Louisiana culinary creation, gumbo knows no boundaries. It graces the tables of the most humble and the most elegant homes and restaurants. There is something about enjoying a bowl of gumbo with another that arouses a certain kinship and bond. You are sharing more than a meal. You are sharing a tradition, a storied history, and a delicious culinary representation of many cultures merging.

YIELD:
17 - 20 servings

INGREDIENTS:
For the Roux:
1 c tapioca flour
1/2 c arrowroot flour
1/2 c coconut flour
1 c palm shortening

2 c onion, chopped
1 c celery, chopped
1/2 c bell pepper, chopped
8 c chicken stock
3 c water, divided equally
1 T salt (adjust based
on ingredients)
1 1/2 t black pepper
1/2 t cayenne
4 t paprika
1 t oregano (finely ground)
1 lb andouille sausage
1 lb smoked sausage
1 lb boneless and skinless
chicken thighs
1 quart smothered okra or
20 oz. frozen cut okra, thawed

PROCESS:
Over a medium-high heat melt palm shortening. Once melted add in flour mixture and stir quickly to combine. Mixture will be very thick. Cook for 7 minutes, stirring frequently, every minute or so.

At this stage your roux will have loosened up a bit and should be easier to stir. Lower heat to medium and continue to cook for another 15 - 20 minutes, stirring almost constantly. Your roux should be the color of a medium or dark brown paper bag to allow for good toasting of the flour.

Once desired color is achieved remove pot from heat and rapidly stir in the holy trinity (onions, celery, and bell pepper) plus 1 c of water. Mixture will become very gelatinous and will sizzle and smoke as vegetables cook.

Add broth or stock and 1 c water. Bring to a boil, stirring occasionally or until roux thins out and clumps disappear. When mixture begins to boil add seasonings and boil for another five minutes.

Lower heat to medium and add chicken thighs and okra. If using frozen okra be sure it is thawed first. Simmer for 20 minutes, stirring frequently to keep okra from sticking. Next, add the andouille and cook for another 10 minutes.

Chicken thighs should begin to fall apart when done. Add 1 c of water if you'd like a thinner consistency at this stage. Adjust seasoning to your liking.

Serve over rice if desired and garnish with fresh green onions and hot sauce to taste. Enjoy!

Notes: Double your roux recipe. Reserve and freeze half of it and your next gumbo will be a breeze!

About this Recipe
PALEO / DAIRY FREE / EGG FREE / NUT FREE / GLUTEN FREE

SPRINGTIME SPAGHETTI

This fresh take on a pasta will leave you satisfied without the carb overload sensation.

YIELD:

6 - 8 servings

INGREDIENTS:

1 four lb spaghetti squash

1 lb wild caught shrimp, peeled

4 oz. diced prosciutto or ham

10 oz. shiitake mushrooms

1 lb frozen organic peas
(or fresh if available!)

2 c baby carrots,
sliced diagonally

2 T shallots, minced

2 t Italian seasoning

3 T olive oil

salt and pepper to taste

Fresh dill, for garnish

PROCESS:

Preheat oven to 450 and cut spaghetti squash in half lengthwise. Place both halves flesh side down in a baking dish filled with enough water to submerge the cut edge. Bake for 30 – 40 minutes depending on size or until fork tender.

Bring a small pot of water to boil and add peas and carrots. Bring back to a boil and reduce heat and simmer for 7 - 10 minutes.

Meanwhile, heat 1T olive oil in a skillet over medium heat. Saute shrimp 2-4 minutes on each side depending on size. Remove from skillet and set aside.

Saute shallots in 1 T olive oil until translucent, about 6 minutes.

Remove squash from oven and discard cooking water. Carefully "Spaghetti" the squash with a fork.

Strain any cooking water from vegetables and set aside.

Add all previously cooked ingredients to skillet on low heat with 1 T of olive oil.

Toss in prosciutto, Italian seasoning, salt and pepper, and additional olive oil if desired. Mix thoroughly with tongs and allow all ingredients to heat.

Garnish with fresh dill and enjoy!

*Notes: Make your spaghetti squash ahead of time or use an electric pressure cooker to drastically cut down the cooking time! *To make this recipe AIP just leave out the black pepper.*

About this Recipe
PALEO / DAIRY FREE / EGG FREE / AIP / KETOGENIC / COCONUT FREE / NUT FREE / GLUTEN FREE*

POTAGE AU CAJUN

This satisfying soup, or potage, was inspired by Emeril Lagasse's Sweet Potato and Andouille Soup recipe. I salute you, Mr. Lagasse, and your culinary talent amazes me. My Mom and I have modified this recipe over the years and I've revamped it again for this book. Cauliflower steps in for the potatoes and makes for a nutrient-packed and low-carb comforting dish that still boasts a creamy and luxurious texture. You won't believe how well spicy andouille sausage pairs with the flavors of savory roasted cauliflower. You'll notice the yield for this recipe is large. That's intentional as it freezes and reheats like a dream.

YIELD:
10 - 14 servings

INGREDIENTS:
2 1/2 lbs cauliflower florets (typically 3 small heads)
2 T + 1 T avocado oil
1 1/2 lbs andouille, chopped
2 c onion, chopped
1 c celery, chopped
1/2 c bell pepper, chopped
4-5 garlic cloves, minced
6 c chicken bone broth
1 1/2 t + 1/4 t + 1/4 t salt
2 t smoked paprika
1/4 - 1/2 t cayenne pepper
2 bay leaves
2 sprigs fresh thyme or
2 t dried thyme
Green onions, for garnish

PROCESS:
Coat cauliflower florets with 1 T oil and ¼ t salt. Place on a sheet pan and roast for 25 minutes at 350 degrees F. They should be beginning to turn brown on the edges and easily pierced with a fork.

Meanwhile, brown chopped andouille in a large stockpot over medium heat, about 8 minutes. Stir a few times to ensure even caramelization. Once well-caramelized, remove sausage from the pot carefully and allow to drain. Take care to leave the fat that has rendered out in the pot.

Add remaining 2 T of avocado oil to the stockpot and increase heat to medium-high. Add in holy trinity and ¼ t salt. Saute for 7 minutes or until onions are translucent. Add garlic and saute for another minute.

While the holy trinity cooks, transfer roasted cauliflower to your high-powered blender container with 3 cups of broth. Blend until very smooth. You may need to work in two batches.

Add mixture to your stockpot along with remaining broth, seasonings, and herbs. Bring to a boil then reduce heat to medium low and allow soup to simmer for 20 minutes.

Remove bay leaves and thyme sprigs from the pot. If desired, you can blend soup a second time (in batches) to achieve an extra-creamy consistency. Garnish soup with andouille and chopped green onions.

*Notes: Potato Lover? Use ½ lb - 1 lb of baked potato or baked sweet potato in place of cauliflower. *To make soup vegetarian substitute vegetable broth for chicken broth and omit andouille. *If you can tolerate dairy, top with grated smoked gouda cheese.*

About this Recipe
PALEO / DAIRY FREE / EGG FREE / COCONUT FREE / NUT FREE / VEGETARIAN* / GLUTEN FREE*

SHRIMP AND ANDOUILLE GUMBO

In Louisiana it's a serious offense to say someone else's gumbo is better than your mom's. Lucky for me my mom's gumbo is truly amazing. Shrimp and Andouille was always my favorite combo. I remember returning home from the Sugarcane Festival parade when I was about 10. When I stepped onto the end of our driveway the unmistakable smell of roux hit me and I knew that Mom was making a gumbo. The slightly cooler weather had just set in (In South Louisiana we rejoice when temps drop below 80 degrees) yet I had an instant feeling of warmth inside knowing that we would all enjoy gumbo together that night.

YIELD:
17 - 20 servings

INGREDIENTS:
For the Roux:
1 c tapioca flour
½ c arrowroot flour
½ c coconut flour
1 c palm shortening
1 c water

Other:
2 c onion
1 c celery
1/2 c bell pepper
8 c chicken bone broth or stock
2 c water, divided equally
1 T salt (adjust based
on ingredients)
1 1/2 t black pepper
1/2 t cayenne
3 t paprika
1 t oregano (finely ground)
1 ½ t garlic powder
1.5 lbs andouille sausage
1.5 lbs raw shrimp, peeled
and deveined
1 quart smothered okra or about
20oz. frozen cut okra

PROCESS:
Over a medium-high heat melt palm shortening. Once melted add in flour mixture and stir quickly to combine. Mixture will be very thick. Cook for 7 minutes, stirring frequently, every minute or so.

At this stage your roux will have loosened up a bit and should be easier to stir. Lower heat to medium and continue to cook for another 15 - 20 minutes, stirring almost constantly. Your roux should be the color of a medium or dark brown paper bag to allow for good toasting of the flour.

Once desired color is achieved remove pot from heat and rapidly stir in the holy trinity (onions, celery, and bell pepper) plus 1 c of water. Mixture will become very gelatinous and will sizzle and smoke as vegetables cook.

Add broth or stock and 1 c water. Bring to a boil, stirring occasionally or until roux thins out and clumps disappear. When mixture begins to boil add seasonings and boil for another five minutes.

Lower heat to medium and add andouille and okra. If using frozen okra be sure it is thawed first. Continue cooking for 20 - 30 minutes, stirring frequently to keep okra from sticking.

Add 1 c of water if you'd like a thinner consistency at this stage. Lastly add raw shrimp and allow to cook for another 7 - 10 minutes. Adjust seasoning to your liking.

Serve over rice if desired and garnish with fresh green onions and hot sauce to taste. Enjoy!

Notes: The level of seasoning needed will depend heavily upon how much spice your andouille contains. Note that your seasoning will typically intensify overnight.

About this Recipe
PALEO / DAIRY FREE / EGG FREE / NUT FREE / GLUTEN FREE

PASTALAYA

aka Jambalaya "Pasta"

While I can devour jambalaya with the best of them, I sometimes want a less carb–heavy option. Enter Spaghetti Squash. Now I realize that spaghetti squash will not be a true comparison for perfectly tender yet toothsome rice or even a nice pasta for a "pastalaya"... but if you want to give your waistline a break, I think you'll be impressed with this dish.

YIELD:
6 - 8 servings

INGREDIENTS:
1 medium spaghetti squash, about 5 cups cooked al dente
2 c onion, chopped
1 c celery, chopped
1/2 green bell pepper, chopped
1 lb andouille sausage, sliced
1 lb shrimp
1 T tomato paste
1/4 c chicken stock
1 T olive oil
green onions, for garnish

Seasoning Blend:
1 t salt
1/4 t black pepper
3/4 t paprika
1/8 t chili powder
1/4 t garlic powder
1/4 t oregano
1/8 - 1/4 t of cayenne

In a large skillet, brown andouille in olive oil over a medium heat, about 7 minutes. Remove from pan.

Add in holy trinity (onions, celery, and bell pepper) and 1t of seasoning blend. Cook until onions are tender and translucent, about 7 minutes. Add in garlic and cook for another 2 minutes.

Add in stock, shrimp, tomato paste, and 1/2 t seasoning blend. Cook for approximately another 5 minutes or until shrimp are pink and firm.

Finally, add back in the sausage and spaghetti squash. Add in the remaining seasoning blend and cook for another 2 minutes to ensure flavors meld together.

Serve and enjoy!

Notes: This is a great use for pre-cooked spaghetti squash. An electric pressure cooker cuts down your spaghetti squash cook time significantly.

About this Recipe
PALEO / DAIRY FREE / EGG FREE / KETOGENIC / COCONUT FREE / NUT FREE / GLUTEN FREE

FISH COUBION

My grandmother on my mom's side, Mom-mon, had an army to feed. With 8 children and two in-laws her cooking load was never light. If a friend or family member caught a large drum fish in the nearby Vermilion Bay, my Mom-mon would make a big pot of coubion (pronounced coo-bee-yawn) to feed the family. Although many Cajuns have their own adaptation of the word, this dish has a French origin and in most places is spelled "courtbouillon".

YIELD:
12 - 14 servings

INGREDIENTS:
1/2 c butter
(substitute ghee or palm shortening if desired)
2/3 c arrowroot flour
1/3 c tapioca flour
2 c onion, chopped
1 c celery, chopped
1/2 c bell pepper, chopped
5 cloves garlic, minced
4 c seafood stock
(or chicken stock)
14.5 oz. can diced tomatoes
14 oz. strained tomatoes
1 1/2 t + 1/2 t salt
1 t pepper
1 t paprika
1/2 t cayenne
1 t thyme
2 lbs white fish
(like catfish or cod)
2 T green onions, for garnish
2 T fresh parsley, for garnish

Hot sauce, to taste

PROCESS:
In a stock pot or dutch oven, make a dark blonde roux by cooking butter with flour over a medium-high heat. Stir very frequently until the mixture liquefies and is the color of a medium paper bag.

Add in holy trinity and garlic, stirring quickly for 1 minute.

Add in stock, diced tomatoes, and seasonings (reserving 1/2 t salt for fish). Stir to the bottom of the pot to scrape up any debris. Bring mixture to a boil.

Reduce heat to medium and simmer for 30 minutes uncovered.

Sprinkle 1/2 t salt over the fish.

Reduce heat to low and add fish, allowing it to cook for 5 minutes, or until it flakes easily with a fork.

Finish with fresh parsley and green onions. Adjust seasoning and add hot sauce if desired. Serve over rice.

Notes: While catfish is a popular coubion ingredient, you can use any white and flaky fish available to you. You can also experiment with other types of seafood.

About this Recipe
PALEO / DAIRY FREE / EGG FREE / COCONUT FREE / NUT FREE / GLUTEN FREE*

Entrees

cleansoutherncuisine.com

CRAB CAKES

When I moved away from the state of Louisiana I couldn't find a single restaurant that did crab cakes "right". Louisiana style crab cakes (with the holy trinity of course!) became one of my specialties that friends requested often. Flaxseed meal steps in for the breadcrumbs in my original recipe and ups the nutritional ante.

YIELD:
20 crab cakes

INGREDIENTS:
1 1/2 c onion, chopped
1 c celery, chopped
1/2 c bell pepper, chopped
2 T oil with high smoke point
(like coconut* or avocado)
2/3 c flaxseed meal
1/3 c mayonnaise
2 eggs
1/2 c green onions, chopped
1/4 c parsley, chopped
2 lbs lump crabmeat
(if previously frozen be sure to drain out any excess moisture)

Seasoning Blend:
2 1/2 t salt
1 1/2 t paprika
1 1/2 t black pepper
1 t garlic powder
1/2 t cayenne

Flour Blend:
4 T arrowroot flour
4 T tapioca flour
1 1/2 t seasoning blend
1/2 t salt

1/2 c coconut or avocado oil
for pan frying

PROCESS:
Saute "holy trinity" (onions, bell pepper, celery) in 2 T oil for 6-8 minutes, until onions are translucent. Allow to cool.

Once cool, place sautéed vegetables in a mixing bowl and stir in the following ingredients: flaxseed meal, mayonnaise, eggs, green onions, parsley, and seasoning blend. Reserve 1 1/2 t seasoning blend for flour coating.

Gently fold in crab meat, until just combined. Using about 1/3 cup of the mixture form a cake approximately 3/4" thick. Repeat.

Lay out cakes on parchment paper and dust both sides lightly with flour blend patting gently to make sure cakes are evenly coated.
Heat 2 T oil in a skillet and pan fry cakes for 5 minutes on each side, or until the exterior is lightly browned and slightly crisp.

Place on a paper towel lined plate to drain.

Enjoy with remoulade sauce, pg 91.

Notes: You may need to change out or replenish cooking oil as you go. You can make the crab cake mixture and even shape them a day ahead. Just dust with flour right before cooking.

About this Recipe
PALEO / DAIRY FREE / COCONUT FREE / NUT FREE / GLUTEN FREE*

SMOKY CHICKEN SALAD

This chicken salad is best made with grilled chicken for a layer of smokiness. I opt for less mayonnaise as I like the other ingredients to shine through. This is not your typical southern mayonnaise-laden country club chicken salad. It's chunky, fresh, light, and totally satisfying. Belgian Endives are a great low-carb "vehicle" for this chicken salad.

YIELD:
3 - 4 servings

INGREDIENTS:
1 lb grilled chicken breasts, chopped into about ½" cubes
1 c red seedless grapes, halved
1/2 c toasted chopped pecans
1/3 c celery, chopped fine
2 t fresh tarragon leaves, chopped
3/4 t salt
1/4 t pepper
1/4 c basic mayonnaise
(see page 105 for my recipe)

Marinade:
2 t garlic, minced
3/4 t salt
1 T lemon juice
1/2 t paprika
1/2 t smoked paprika
1/4 t cayenne pepper
2 T oil

PROCESS:
Marinate chicken for at least 30 minutes or up to overnight before grilling.

Stir first 7 ingredients together in a medium sized bowl.

Last gently stir in mayonnaise until everything is lightly coated.

Enjoy!

Notes: You can even turn your leftover grilled chicken into this delicious meal! If you are short on time use a rotisserie chicken. It won't be smoky but it will be delicious!

About this Recipe
PALEO / DAIRY FREE / COCONUT FREE / GLUTEN FREE

SALMON CROQUETTES

Canned fish is not exactly an elegant meal offering. However, this recipe easily transforms it into something you could serve your guests.

YIELD:

12 salmon cakes

INGREDIENTS:

6 six oz. cans wild caught pink salmon

2 eggs

1 c red bell pepper, chopped fine

1 c green onions, chopped

1/4 c shallots, chopped fine (optional)

3 T parsley, chopped

1 t salt

1 t garlic powder

1 t black pepper

1/4 t cayenne

2 T golden flax meal (optional)

2 T avocado oil, for pan frying

PROCESS:

Open and drain all cans.

Transfer salmon to a medium sized mixing bowl and stir in eggs, vegetables, seasonings, and flax until well combined.

Using a large ice cream scoop for consistency, make 12 cakes and flatten them.

Heat oil in a large skillet over medium heat. Cook salmon croquettes for 4 minutes on each side or until well browned.

Notes: Serve these with my Seafood Loving Sauce (pg 88) and a side of roasted asparagus for a quick and delicious dinner.

About this Recipe
PALEO / DAIRY FREE / KETOGENIC / COCONUT FREE / NUT FREE / GLUTEN FREE

MINI TURKEY MEATLOAVES

Individually portioned mini meatloaves are convenient and lessen cooking time, making this recipe a cinch! They are also perfectly portioned for leftovers or lunches on the go. Smoky Spanish Sauce (pg 95) is the perfect complement.

YIELD:

12 mini meatloaves

INGREDIENTS:

3 carrots
(about 2 cups)

2 medium yellow onions
(about 3 cups)

1 T coconut oil

2 large eggs

1/2 t apple cider vinegar

2 t dried basil

1 t dried thyme

3 lbs ground turkey

4 T golden flaxseed meal

3 T organic tomato paste
(from a glass jar if possible)

1 1/2 t + 1/2 t salt

2 t + 1/2 t black pepper

1 t white pepper

3 t paprika

PROCESS:

Chop onions and carrots extra fine and sauté in coconut oil, 1/2 t salt and 1/2 t pepper until translucent, about 7 - 8 minutes. Remove from heat to cool.

In a small bowl, beat the two eggs and add the cider vinegar and herbs.

Mix ground turkey, flaxseed, tomato paste and remaining seasonings in a medium mixing bowl. Add vegetables and egg mixture and stir well to incorporate.

Shape mixture into twelve 3" x 4" meatloaves and place on a parchment lined baking sheet. Bake at 350 degrees F for 45 minutes or until your meat thermometer reads 165 degrees F.

Notes: You can also make 24 mini meatloaves in muffin pans. Just grease the pan, press and equal amount of the mixture into each slot, and then bake for 30 minutes or until a meat thermometer reads 165 degrees F.

About this Recipe
PALEO / DAIRY FREE / KETOGENIC / NUT FREE / GLUTEN FREE

COCONUT CRUSTED SHRIMP

Savory and slightly sweet? Check. Crispy coating and succulent shrimp? Check. Is your mouth watering yet? If so, dive in for this recipe. You won't be sorry you did! My Kickin' Peach Sauce (pg. 93) is the perfect enhancement for these shrimp.

YIELD:

about 6 servings

INGREDIENTS:

Shrimp:

2 lbs raw shrimp, medium size

1 t salt

1 t pepper

1/2 t garlic powder

1/4 - 1/2 t cayenne

Coating:

1/2 c tapioca flour

1 T coconut flour

1/2 t salt

2 large eggs + 2 T water, beaten

1 1/4 c finely shredded unsweetened coconut

1/4 c golden flaxseed meal

PROCESS:

Set up three bowls: 1 - tapioca flour, coconut flour and salt , whisked together. 2 - eggs and water, beaten. 3 - shredded coconut and flaxseed meal.

Combine seasonings for shrimp and season both sides of shrimp.

Dredge through flour mixture, egg mixture, and finally generously coat in coconut mixture.

Set aside while you heat 2 T of coconut oil in a large skillet. Cook shrimp for 2 - 3 minutes per side over a medium-high heat.

You may need to change out or replenish cooking oil as you go.

Notes: You may need to adjust cooking time depending on the size of your shrimp.

About this Recipe
PALEO / DAIRY FREE / KETOGENIC / NUT FREE / GLUTEN FREE

STUFFED PORK TENDERLOIN

Brandy soaked apricots create a jammy and festive flavor profile. Tender walnuts take the place of breadcrumbs and add richness and texture. This entree is splendidly holiday and special occasion–worthy.

YIELD:
10 - 12 servings

INGREDIENTS:
Two 1 1/2 lb pork tenderloins, butterflied

1 cup dried apricots, soaked

1 cup walnuts, soaked

1/2 c brandy

1 c water

4 oz prosciutto

1 T thyme

1 t salt

1/2 t black pepper

1/2 t garlic powder

1 T dijon mustard

1/2 t salt

1/2 t black pepper

PROCESS:
Soak apricots in brandy overnight.

Soak walnuts in water overnight.

Drain apricots and walnuts, reserving leftover brandy.

Chop apricots, walnuts, and prosciutto into small pieces, about 1 cm or less. Place in small bowl.

Add thyme and seasonings, stirring to combine stuffing. Lay out butterflied loins and coat each evenly with 1/2 T mustard. Spread stuffing evenly between two loins.

Roll up tenderloins, starting with the long side, and secure with butcher's twine every 2 inches or so.

Heat 2 T olive oil in a skillet. Sear over medium heat, about 2 minutes per side.

Bake at 350 degrees F for 30 minutes or until an internal thermometer registers at least 145 degrees.

Allow loins to rest for 10 minutes before slicing and serving.

About this Recipe
PALEO / DAIRY FREE / EGG FREE / COCONUT FREE / GLUTEN FREE

SEAFOOD SALAD

This entree is rich and creamy yet not overly filling. It's an utterly satisfying lunch or dinner any day of the week. If you don't have both shrimp and crab on hand you can just use one or the other.

YIELD:

About 4 servings

INGREDIENTS:

1 lb pre-cooked shrimp, chopped

1/2 lb crabmeat

1 c celery, chopped fine

2 T fresh chives

2 T fresh dill

1/2 t salt

1/4 t pepper

1/2 c mayonnaise

PROCESS:

Combine all ingredients in a bowl and chill until ready to serve.

Garnish with extra fresh dill and chives.

Notes: Enjoy this salad in half of an avocado, serve it atop greens, with my sesame seed crackers (pg 41), or solo!

About this Recipe
PALEO / DAIRY FREE / KETOGENIC / COCONUT FREE / NUT FREE / GLUTEN FREE

CRAWFISH PIE

In Louisiana we are blessed with many meals made up of humble ingredients that come together to create an end result that is truly decadent. When I think of the aroma of crawfish pie wafting from my mother's kitchen, I'm immediately transported back to the warmth of childhood. Just as it was back then, I'm always willing to partake in this dish – even as a leftover.

YIELD:
Two 9" pies

INGREDIENTS:
Roux:
1 c grass fed organic butter
1 c arrowroot flour
1/4 c c tapioca flour
1 - 2 T coconut flour

2 Prepared Pie Crusts
(see page 150 for my recipe)
2 c onion, chopped
1/2 c red bell pepper, chopped
1/2 c celery, chopped
1 c mushrooms, chopped
2 lbs peeled crawfish and fat
2/3 c grass fed organic
heavy cream
3/4 c green onions
1/4 c parsley
3 1/2 t salt
2 t black pepper
4 t paprika
1/2 t - 1 t cayenne pepper
2 1/2 t garlic powder
Tabasco brand hot sauce
to taste, *(optional)*

PROCESS:
Parbake pie crusts for 15 minutes at 350 degrees F.

Meanwhile, melt butter in a large skillet over medium low heat. Add in flours and stir frequently to make a blonde roux.

Add in holy trinity (onions, celery, bell pepper) stirring quickly to allow them to cook, about 30 seconds. Mixture will smoke heavily!

Remove from heat and add in all other ingredients, in order listed. Stir until well combined.

Fill two prepared pie shells.

Bake for 30 minutes at 350 degrees F.

For a more solid consistency allow pies to cool to room temperature before serving.

*Notes: *To make this recipe dairy free substitute 1 c of palm shortening for the butter and 1/3 c mayonnaise for the heavy cream.*

About this Recipe
PALEO / DAIRY FREE / EGG FREE / COCONUT FREE / NUT FREE / GLUTEN FREE*

Sauces, Dips, & Staples

cleansoutherncuisine.com

SEAFOOD LOVING SAUCE

I love to whip up a good sauce with a mayo base. Mayo truly is the mother sauce! This one was born because you sometimes need to dress up a simple seafood dish like baked fish or salmon croquettes. However, It also lends itself to more elegant offerings like crab cakes.

YIELD:

3/4 cup

INGREDIENTS:

1/2 c Basic Mayonnaise
(*pg 105*)

2 T capers, rinsed

1 T whole grain mustard

2 t fresh or dried dill, chopped

Salt and pepper to taste

squeeze of lemon
(*optional*)

PROCESS:

Combine all ingredients and stir well.

Refrigerate for a minimum of one hour.

Notes: This sauce will intensify in saltiness. If you are going to enjoy it right away you may want to add a pinch of salt. If you are making it ahead the capers will impart plenty of salt. You can make this sauce with a store bought mayo but be sure it doesn't contain any canola oil, soy, or sugar. Many store bought mayos of my youth, while they are staples of the South, don't promote good health.

About this Recipe
PALEO / DAIRY FREE / KETOGENIC / COCONUT FREE / NUT FREE / VEGETARIAN / GLUTEN FREE

CSC GLUTEN FREE FLOUR

This flour blend will work as a 1:1 substitution for all purpose wheat flour in most recipes. Using too much gluten free flour can result in gummy baked goods so always sift or at least whisk your flour prior to measuring. Then scoop the flour with a smaller cup or spoon into the desired measuring cup and level it off. These steps will ensure you don't use too much flour.

YIELD:

5 1/4 c flour blend

INGREDIENTS:

2 1/4 c sorghum flour

1 1/4 c brown rice flour

1 c potato starch

1/2 c tapioca flour

1/4 c arrowroot flour

PROCESS:

Sift, measure, and whisk all ingredients together in a large bowl.

Store in airtight container until ready to use.

Notes: To keep this flour fresh for longer store it in the refrigerator for up to 2 months. Allow it to come to room temperature prior to using.

IMPORTANT: For certain baking applications this flour blend can be enhanced. In the place of gluten, xanthan gum can act as a binder and provide structure in recipes. It will give your gluten free baked goods a more traditional texture and keep them from crumbling apart. There are always exceptions but a good rule of thumb is that most baked goods that start as batters (think muffins and cakes) will need about ¼ t xanthan gum per cup of flour and most baked goods that start as a dough (think cookies, pie crust, pizza dough, bread) will need about ½ t - ¾ t xanthan gum per cup of flour. If you are using the flour for a very basic application (think thickening a soup or sauce) there is no need to add xanthan gum.

About this Recipe
VEGAN / DAIRY FREE / EGG FREE / COCONUT FREE / NUT FREE / VEGETARIAN / GLUTEN FREE

REMOULADE SAUCE

One of the most well-known sauces of New Orleans, remoulade, has many different variations. This one is creamy, tangy, and full bodied as I prefer my remoulade sauce to have a mayonnaise base. One of my favorite on-the-go meals is fresh crab meat, tossed in remoulade, and served in half of an avocado. It doesn't get much more delicious or simple than that.

YIELD:

1/2 cup

INGREDIENTS:

6 T mayo

1 T prepared horseradish

2 t dijon mustard

2 t whole grain mustard

2 t ketchup, optional

1 t apple cider vinegar

1/2 t paprika

Pinch of salt

Hot sauce to your liking

PROCESS:

Combine all ingredients in a small bowl and refrigerate.

Allow flavors to marry overnight before using.

Notes: Customize the heat in your remoulade with hot sauce and a pinch of cayenne pepper, if desired. In my family we love to use Tabasco brand Family Reserve Hot Sauce!

About this Recipe
PALEO / DAIRY FREE / KETOGENIC / COCONUT FREE / NUT FREE / VEGETARIAN / GLUTEN FREE

KICKIN' PEACH SAUCE

Sweet and tangy strike a perfect balance in this sauce and red pepper flakes give it a nice kick – hence the name! It's important to find a brand of preserves that doesn't add any sugar as the natural sugar contained in peaches is plentiful. This sauce is the perfect partner to fried seafood but it also pairs well with grilled pork, chicken, or fish. Or upgrade your sandwich by spreading this onto toasted bread.

YIELD:

1/4 cup

INGREDIENTS:

3 T peach preserves

1 T dijon mustard

1/4 t - 1/2 t red pepper flakes

pinch of salt

PROCESS:

Mix together all ingredients in a small bowl
Store in refrigerator for up to a week.

Notes: As is the case with most recipes that use red pepper flakes, this sauce will intensify in heat as you store it.

About this Recipe
VEGAN / PALEO / DAIRY FREE / EGG FREE / COCONUT FREE / NUT FREE / VEGETARIAN / GLUTEN FREE

SMOKY SPANISH SAUCE

Have you ever looked at the ingredient list on a standard ketchup bottle? They typically involve high fructose corn syrup, soybean oil, and "natural flavor". None of these ingredients are kind to our bodies. Enter Smoky Spanish Sauce.... this sauce is a great substitute for ketchup but can also be enjoyed as you would a salsa (try it with plantain chips!), or with grilled meats or meatloaf. The smoked paprika gives this sauce a slightly sophisticated edge.

YIELD:

2/3 cup

INGREDIENTS:

1/2 c strained tomatoes (pureed)

2 t smoked paprika

1/2 t salt

1 t garlic powder

2 t agave nectar

15 - 16 drops fresh lemon juice

cayenne to taste, optional

PROCESS:

Combine all ingredients in a small container and stir until well combined.

Store in refrigerator for up to a week. This sauce is always better the next day.

Notes: Use high quality organic strained tomatoes from a glass jar if possible.

About this Recipe
VEGAN / PALEO / DAIRY FREE / EGG FREE / COCONUT FREE / NUT FREE / VEGETARIAN / GLUTEN FREE

SUNNY DAYS DIP

My middle sister, Jennifer, and I would typically get home from school before the rest of the family. She always concocted great snacks for the two of us. I would sit right on the kitchen counter (sorry Mom!) and we would talk while she whipped up the snack du jour for us. One of our favorites was a dip made of simply of cottage cheese and an herb salt seasoning mixture. We loved to have it with tortilla chips. Ah, the simple pleasures of childhood and being the youngest sibling! Now that I focus on consuming less dairy I've gotten pretty good at concocting snacks and dips myself. This dip relies on soaked cashews to make a creamy hummus–like base and is jam–packed with flavor and protein.

YIELD:

2 1/2 cups

INGREDIENTS:

1 1/2 c raw cashews, soaked

1 T lemon juice

8 oz jar sundried tomatoes in olive oil (do not drain!)

3 T fresh basil

1/2 t salt

1 clove garlic

About 1 c water

1/2 c sliced kalamata olives, optional

PROCESS:

Cover cashews in water and soak for 6 hours or overnight.

Drain cashews.

Place first six ingredients in food processor or high powered blender.

Pulse until crumbles form.

Next blend or process continuously while streaming in water until dip becomes a smooth consistency.

Stir in olives by hand.

Notes: You may need to use more or less water to achieve desired consistency. This is a great make-ahead option as flavors actually improve the day after.

About this Recipe
VEGAN / PALEO / DAIRY FREE / EGG FREE / KETOGENIC / COCONUT FREE / VEGETARIAN / GLUTEN FREE

QUICK GUACAMOLE

My sister-in-law Izabella, who wrote the foreword for this book, is a big fan of guacamole. Sometimes I ask her "what can I bring" and she says guacamole. However, in the throes of a busy week I don't always have time to pull out the molcajete and make the killer guacamole that my friends and family request. This is a minimalist version that takes hardly any time but is still very pleasing to eat. Here you go Izabella – guacamole anytime – no chopping required!

YIELD:

about 1 cup

INGREDIENTS:

1 large hass avocado or
2 small avocados

1 t freshly squeezed lime juice

1/4 t ground white pepper

1/4 t sea salt

PROCESS:

In a small bowl smash avocado flesh until desired consistency is achieved.

Add in salt, white pepper, and lime juice. Stir to combine.

Enjoy!

*Notes: Best consumed fresh! If you are going to store in the refrigerator add a little extra lime juice so the color and taste will be preserved.
To make this recipe AIP simply omit the pepper.

About this Recipe
VEGAN / PALEO / DAIRY FREE / EGG FREE / AIP / KETOGENIC / COCONUT FREE / NUT FREE / VEGETARIAN / GLUTEN FREE*

BELLE BLEND CAJUN SEASONING

Many of us Southerners grew up using a cajun seasoning blend for its convenience. I prefer to make my own so I can ensure the spices are organic and that is doesn't contain any anti-caking agents like silicon dioxide. Throw this seasoning together and sprinkle it on anything to liven it up a bit!

YIELD:
1/4 cup

INGREDIENTS:
1 T salt
(adjust based on ingredients)

1 1/2 t black pepper

1/2 t cayenne

1 T paprika

1 t chili powder

1 t oregano (finely ground)

1 1/2 t garlic powder

1/2 t onion powder

1/2 t dried lemon peel

PROCESS:
Combine all ingredients with a small whisk.

Store in an airtight container out of the sunlight.

Notes: This seasoning is best used within 6 months.

About this Recipe
VEGAN / PALEO / DAIRY FREE / EGG FREE / KETOGENIC / COCONUT FREE / NUT FREE / VEGETARIAN / GLUTEN FREE

CREAMY SATSUMA BASIL DRESSING

Each year I look forward to returning home to South Louisiana for Christmas and spending a sunny winter day picking satsumas. Mind you a winter day in South Louisiana is generally in the 60's which makes this experience even nicer. Satsumas are small citrus fruits that are in season in December. They are easier to peel and contain fewer seeds than oranges. They are also juicier and sweeter making them a perfect base for a sauce or even a savory application.

YIELD:
1 cup

INGREDIENTS:
1/3 c freshly squeezed satsuma juice
2 T dijon mustard
1/2 t salt
1 t honey
1/2 c olive oil
1 T fresh basil, chopped fine
2 t satsuma zest

PROCESS:
Put first four ingredients into blender or food processor and process on lowest setting possible.

Stream in olive oil very slowly to form an emulsion

Add basil and pulse until just chopped.

Add satsuma zest by hand and enjoy!

Notes: Store in refrigerator for up to a week. You can substitute freshly squeezed orange juice for the satsuma juice if need be.

About this Recipe | VEGAN / PALEO / DAIRY FREE / EGG FREE / AIP / COCONUT FREE / NUT FREE / VEGETARIAN / GLUTEN FREE

LEMON POPPYSEED VINAIGRETTE

Often when people are new to a clean eating lifestyle they wonder what they'll replace their store bought salad dressings with. It seems like a time consuming conundrum but most don't realize how quick and easy salad dressings actually are to whip up and how amazing fresh dressing can taste.

YIELD:
2/3 cup

INGREDIENTS:
2 T lemon juice
1 1/2 T dijon mustard
1/2 t salt
1 1/2 T agave nectar

1/2 c olive oil

1/2 t poppyseeds
Zest from half of a lemon

PROCESS:
Put first four ingredients in blender and blend on lowest setting possible.

Stream in olive oil very slowly to form an emulsion.

Stir in zest and poppy seeds by hand.

Enjoy!

Notes: Store in refrigerator for up to a week.

About this Recipe | VEGAN / PALEO / DAIRY FREE / EGG FREE / COCONUT FREE / NUT FREE / VEGETARIAN / GLUTEN FREE

BASIC MAYONNAISE

Upon trying homemade mayonnaise, most people, even if they've never liked the store bought variety, fall in love. Although there are some mayos on the market today with clean ingredients they tend to be a little pricey and there is absolutely no substitute for homemade mayo. Mayo can be used as a base for salad dressings, sauces, and a substitute for heavy cream in many recipes. The keys to your mayo success are: 1 – All ingredients must be room temperature. 2 – Use a light oil with a mild taste. Do not use Extra Virgin Olive Oil for this! 3 – A healthy dose of patience.

YIELD:

1 1/2 cups

INGREDIENTS:

1/4 c extra light olive oil
or avocado oil

1 egg

1T lemon juice

1 t dijon mustard

1/4 t salt

3/4 c extra light olive oil
or avocado oil

PROCESS:

Blender:
Place first 5 ingredients in your blender or food processor. Blend or pulse for 45 seconds to ensure ingredients incorporate.

Next, using a low blender or processor speed, continuously stream in oil as slowly as possible without interruptions.

When mixture has emulsified you will hear less "crackling" sounds. You aren't done yet!

Continue to stream the oil slowly. It should take you 2 - 3 minutes to pour all of the oil out.

Turn off blender or processor as soon as all oil has been streamed.

Refrigerate immediately and enjoy!

Notes: With this recipe patience is a virtue! If you are using a Vitamix blender 2 is the speed to stick with throughout. If using a food processor try the low setting. Your mayonnaise will last until the expiration date of your eggs.

About this Recipe
PALEO / DAIRY FREE / KETOGENIC / COCONUT FREE / NUT FREE / VEGETARIAN / GLUTEN FREE

Sides & Salads

cleansoutherncuisine.com

CARROT SALAD

Need some variety in the salad department? Sweet and crunchy carrots, with a few other ingredients for texture, will make this the least boring salad of your week.

YIELD:
5 - 7 servings

INGREDIENTS:
4 c finely grated carrots

3/4 c dried cranberries

1/2 c mayonnaise

1/4 c sunflower seeds, roasted and salted

PROCESS:
Grate carrots in food processor and place in a refrigerator-suitable bowl.

Stir mayonnaise and dried cranberries into grated carrots.

Refrigerate at least 30 minutes prior to serving.

Add sunflower seeds just before serving.

Notes: This salad will keep in the refrigerator for up to a week.

About this Recipe
PALEO / DAIRY FREE / COCONUT FREE / NUT FREE / VEGETARIAN / GLUTEN FREE

TWICE BAKED SWEET POTATOES

This hearty side is almost a meal unto itself. Savory mushrooms and bacon play nicely with the natural sweetness of the potatoes.

YIELD:

6 servings

INGREDIENTS:

6 medium sized sweet potatoes

1 c fried and chopped bacon pieces (about 10 slices of bacon)

3 T green onions, chopped

1 1/2 c of white mushrooms, chopped and sauteed

1 1/2 t salt

1/2 t garlic powder

2 T ghee or grass-fed butter, optional

1/2 c smoked gouda cheese, optional

PROCESS:

Bake potatoes for about 45 minutes at 400 degrees, or until tender when pierced with a fork.

Make a 1″ deep lengthwise cut in each potato, leaving an inch or so at each end.

Squeeze the two ends together to widen your slit.

Spoon out potato flesh, leaving skin and a thin layer of potato in tact to form a shell.

Transfer all flesh to a mixing bowl and repeat for each potato.

Add seasonings and optional ghee or butter. Mash potatoes until creamy.

Next stir in bacon, mushrooms, and green onions.

Transfer equal amounts of filling back into potato shells.

Top with smoked gouda cheese if desired. Place potatoes back in oven for 15 minutes.

Remove and garnish with additional green onion before serving.

*Notes: *Simply omit the bacon to make this recipe Vegetarian.*

About this Recipe
PALEO / EGG FREE / COCONUT FREE / NUT FREE / VEGETARIAN / GLUTEN FREE*

SCALLOPED POTATOES

Luxuriously layered scalloped potatoes... perhaps one of the queens of comfort food. However, for those who can't tolerate dairy these are a distant daydream... not any longer! You could serve these potatoes to any guest and they'd never guess the dish is non-dairy. It has got all of the richness, all of the creaminess, and all of the comfort.

YIELD:
10 - 12 servings

INGREDIENTS:
1 T olive oil
4 lbs yukon gold potatoes, sliced ¼" thickness at most

Seasoning:
1/2 t nutmeg
1 1/2 t salt
1/2 t black pepper

Sauce:
1 T olive oil
1 shallot, minced
2 cloves of garlic, minced
1/2 t salt
1 3/4 c low sodium chicken broth
1 T arrowroot powder
2/3 c mayonnaise (pg. 105)
1/3 c non dairy milk
(cashew or macadamia)

PROCESS:
Combine salt, pepper, and nutmeg to make seasoning.

Coat a 9" X 13" baking dish with olive oil.

Slice potatoes and layer them into baking dish, sprinkling seasoning mixture on every layer as you go. Set aside.

In a small saucepan, saute shallots and garlic in 1 T of olive oil, over a medium heat, for about 4 minutes. Season with 1/2 t of salt.

Add in chicken broth and bring to a boil. Reduce to simmer and whisk in non dairy milk and mayonnaise.

Thicken with 1 T arrowroot powder and continue to whisk until consistency of heavy cream is reached. Remove from heat.

Pour liquid into dish so that potatoes are submerged.

Bake 350 degrees F, covered, for 1 hour.

Remove cover and broil for 5 - 7 minutes or until the top layer is just browned and bubbly.

*Notes: While Russet potatoes are the most starchy and will make the thickest sauce, I prefer the taste of Yukon Gold. *To make this dish vegetarian sub vegetable broth for chicken broth.*

About this Recipe
PALEO / DAIRY FREE / COCONUT FREE / VEGETARIAN / GLUTEN FREE*

MOST AMAZING BRUSSELS

One particular member of my extended family, whom shall remain unnamed, doesn't get overly excited about food. When I made these brussel sprouts for him he exclaimed that these were "the best I've ever had!". In other words, these are not the palid boiled brussel sprouts that many of us dreaded as youths. When prepared this way you'll wind up with a slightly crispy and charred exterior. Sweet and tangy ingredients harmonize perfectly to create a craveable side dish. Although, these really do feel more like a treat than a vegetable side dish. Beware that two brussel–loving diners can easily polish off this recipe. If you fall into this category go ahead and double it.

YIELD:
3 - 4 servings

INGREDIENTS:

1 lb brussel sprouts

½ t salt

¼ t black pepper

¼ t nutmeg

3 T olive oil

2 t apple cider vinegar

2 t balsamic vinegar

2 t maple syrup

1 t dijon mustard

Optional toppings:
Goat cheese crumbles

Toasted chopped pecans

PROCESS:

Place a rimmed baking sheet in your oven before turning it on. Allow the baking sheet to remain there while the oven preheats to 425 degrees F.

Meanwhile, wash sprouts thoroughly and remove any stems. Removing the first two leaves or so if dirty, halve each sprout lengthwise.

In a mixing bowl combine salt, black pepper, nutmeg, olive oil, and apple cider vinegar. Toss the sprouts in this mixture until well coated.

Carefully remove the hot baking sheet from the oven and pour the sprouts onto it. They will sizzle. Working quickly with a pair of kitchen tongs, ensure most of the sprouts are cut side down and space them out.

Roast for 18 - 25 minutes at 425 degrees F. While the sprouts roast, combine balsamic vinegar, maple syrup, and mustard to make a glaze.

Remove sprouts from oven and immediately drizzle with glaze. Toss gently to coat if desired. Add any optional toppings you'd like and serve immediately.

*Notes: *For Vegan and Dairy Free omit goat cheese. *For AIP omit nutmeg and black pepper. *For Keto omit maple syrup. *For Nut Free omit pecans.*

About this Recipe
VEGAN / PALEO / DAIRY FREE* / EGG FREE / AIP* / KETOGENIC* / COCONUT FREE / NUT FREE* / VEGETARIAN / GLUTEN FREE*

LAYERED SPINACH SALAD

When we visit my parents in Cajun country, my husband Robert always complains that he can't find a "real" salad anywhere. Having grown up in Europe with the benefit of more flavorful produce, he doesn't see the point of iceberg lettuce with its lack of flavor and little nutritional value. He got into the habit of asking restaurant staff if they have "real" salads, which is pretty funny to the rest of us. Robert, this "real" salad is for you honey.

YIELD:
6 - 8 servings

INGREDIENTS:
5 oz. clamshell of fresh spinach

10 oz. frozen peas, thawed

1 - 8 oz. can of water chestnuts, chopped

Dressing
(see ingredients below)

3/4 c bacon bits (nitrate free)

1/2 c red bell pepper, chopped

1/2 c green onions, chopped

For Dressing:
1 1/4 c pimento mayonnaise
(visit website for recipe)

1/4 t salt

1/4 t black pepper

1/4 t dried oregano

PROCESS:
In a glass bowl, layer ingredients in the order listed.

Refrigerate until ready to serve

Notes: This salad can be made ahead and stored for up to 3 days. If you use pimento mayo do not add the dressing until just before eating. However, traditional mayonnaise will be thicker and can be added in ahead of time and stored.

• *PHOTO ON PAGE 107*

About this Recipe
PALEO / DAIRY FREE / COCONUT FREE / NUT FREE / VEGETARIAN / GLUTEN FREE

QUICK PICKLED (BÁNH MÌ) VEGGIES

While living in New Orleans, I fell in love with Bánh mì which is the Vietnamese take on the po'boy (sandwich). This blend of vegetables is traditionally found fresh on a Bánh mì po'boy along with sliced jalapenos, fresh cilantro, and some sort of savory meat. Use these crisp quick pickled veggies to liven any sandwich or salad...or just enjoy them on their own.

YIELD:

3 quart sized canning jars

INGREDIENTS:

2 c rice wine vinegar
or white vinegar

1 c apple cider vinegar

3 c water

3 T salt

5 c carrot, grated (1 1/2 lbs)

2 1/2 c radish, grated (one large)

2 1/2 c cucumber, grated
(one large)

2 jalapenos, sliced thin (optional)

15 whole peppercorns

3 garlic cloves

PROCESS:

In a medium saucepan heat both vinegars, water, and salt until salt is dissolved. Remove from heat and allow to cool.

Grate or cut vegetables into matchsticks and pack tightly into 3 quart sized canning jars.

Distribute peppercorns, garlic cloves, and jalapeno slices evenly between the jars.

Pour warm or room temperature (not hot) liquid into jars and top with lids.

Ensure jars are room temperature before refrigerating.

Refrigerate and enjoy for up to a month.

Notes: You can enjoy these vegetables as soon as 30 minutes after assembling. If you don't have a daikon radish on hand any sort of radish will work well.

About this Recipe
VEGAN / PALEO / DAIRY FREE / EGG FREE / KETOGENIC / COCONUT FREE / NUT FREE / VEGETARIAN / GLUTEN FREE

CARROTS, PARSNIPS, AND PARSLEY

This side dish opts for parsnips over potatoes.   Parsnips are embraced by quite a few clean-eating lifestyles as they are rich in vitamins as well as manganese and phosphorus.   When mashed they can closely resemble potatoes and have a similar texture.

YIELD:

6 - 8 servings

INGREDIENTS:

4 c carrots, chopped

3 c parsnips, chopped

2 T parsley, chopped

2 T ghee

1 t + 1/2 t sea salt

PROCESS:

Peel and chop carrots and parsnips to approximately the same size.

Place vegetables in a large pot. Cover with water until vegetables are submerged under 2 inches of water.

Add 1 t of salt and bring to a boil.

Lower heat to a gentle boil and cook for about 10 minutes, or until vegetables are fork-tender.

Drain water and mix in chopped parsley, ghee, and 1/2 t salt.

*Notes: *Use coconut oil or olive oil in place of ghee to make this recipe Vegan.*

About this Recipe

VEGAN / PALEO / DAIRY FREE / EGG FREE / AIP / COCONUT FREE / NUT FREE / VEGETARIAN / GLUTEN FREE*

ROASTED ASPARAGUS SALAD

Toss this salad together in a snap and enjoy its clean and refreshing flavors. This is a great side to counter the richness of summer barbeque.

YIELD:
6 - 8 servings

INGREDIENTS:
One bunch asparagus
(trimmed, roasted, cooled)

2 c chopped tomatoes or
halved cherry tomatoes

1 large cucumber, sliced

1 bell pepper, chopped

2 T fresh dill, minced

1 t fresh mint, minced

1/2 t salt

Lemon Poppyseed Dressing
(page 99)

PROCESS:
Lightly roast asparagus for 8 - 12 minutes at
425 degrees F. Cut stalks into thirds once cool.

Prepare and toss together all vegetables, herbs,
and salt.

Serve immediately or refrigerate until ready
to serve.

Dress salad just before serving.

*Notes: Short on time? This salad can be
tossed with oil and vinegar instead of the
complimentary dressing.*

About this Recipe
VEGAN / PALEO / DAIRY FREE / EGG FREE / KETOGENIC / COCONUT FREE / NUT FREE / VEGETARIAN / GLUTEN FREE

Biscuits & Breads

cleansoutherncuisine.com

BELLE OF THE BALL BISCUITS

The biscuit – a southern dinner table necessity. These fluffy and undetectably gluten free and dairy free biscuits will be the most coveted item on your dinner table, hence the title. No one will believe you if you let them in on the secret. If you can tolerate dairy, feel free to use butter in place of the ghee. Either way, you'll find these biscuits really are the "Belle of the Ball" at any meal.

YIELD:

10 biscuits

INGREDIENTS

2 c CSC gluten free flour
(pg 89)

2 1/4 t baking powder

3/4 t salt

2 t xanthan gum

2/3 c ghee, frozen for
30 minutes to harden

1/2 c cashew milk (unsweetened)

2 eggs

1 T ghee, melted

PROCESS:

Place ghee in the freezer for 30 minutes to harden.

Combine first four ingredients in a mixing bowl. Using a pastry blender or fork, cut ghee into flour blend until there are small crumbs.

Whisk together eggs and milk and pour into dry ingredients.

Stir just until a dough forms.

Cover and refrigerate for 30 minutes to allow flour to absorb moisture. Meanwhile preheat oven to 375 degrees F.

Using a muffin scoop or large ice cream scoop, transfer dough onto parchment lined baking sheet.

Brush each biscuit with melted ghee to "seal" in the moisture.

Bake for 12 - 14 minutes.

*Notes: Be sure not to skip any of the steps as this will ensure you wind up with the appropriate texture and a moist and buttery biscuit. *If you are concerned about a nut allergy you can substitute full-fat coconut milk for the cashew milk but the taste is not as neutral.*

About this Recipe
DAIRY FREE / COCONUT FREE / NUT FREE / VEGETARIAN / GLUTEN FREE*

CARAMELIZED ONION AND ROSEMARY BISCUITS

Since the first time I caramelized onions I've had an absolute love affair with the preparation. They once became the favorite side on the Thanksgiving table at my sister-in-law's house. Due to a miscommunication, my husband and I each added salt to the onions as they cooked. Of all the elaborate sides and casseroles the double salted caramelized onions were the talk of the table. Caramelizing onions brings out both the sweet and savory flavors. Pair them with piney rosemary and it's a match made in biscuit heaven.

YIELD:
10 biscuits

INGREDIENTS:
2 c CSC gluten free flour
(*pg 89*)

2 1/4 t baking powder

3/4 t salt

2 t xanthan gum

2/3 c ghee

1/2 c caramelized onions,
chopped small
(see recipe on website)

1 1/2 T fresh rosemary, minced

1/2 c cashew milk (unsweetened)

2 eggs

1 T ghee, melted

PROCESS:
Place ghee in the freezer for 30 minutes to harden.

Combine first four ingredients in a mixing bowl.

Using a pastry blender or fork cut ghee into flour blend until there are small crumbs.

Whisk in rosemary and caramelized onions, ensuring onions don't stick together too much.

Whisk together eggs and milk and pour into dry ingredients.

Stir until a dough forms.

Cover and refrigerate for 30 minutes to allow flour to absorb moisture.

Using a muffin scoop or large ice cream scoop transfer dough onto parchment lined baking sheet.

Brush each biscuit with melted ghee to "seal" in the moisture.

Bake at 375 for 12 - 14 minutes.

Notes: To switch things up try adding freshly grated cheese and chives instead of caramelized onions and rosemary. You can experiment with many combinations to make these biscuits interesting.

About this Recipe
DAIRY FREE / COCONUT FREE / NUT FREE* / VEGETARIAN / GLUTEN FREE

SEEDED FLATBREAD

This flatbread has some distinct assets. For one, it's the least time consuming bread you'll ever make and you don't even have to turn on the oven! Secondly, it's high in protein and nutrient-rich thanks to almond flour. Caraway seeds give it a delicate rye flavor but you can experiment with other seeds or herbs as well.

YIELD:
three 6" flatbreads

INGREDIENTS:
1 c almond flour
1/2 c arrowroot flour
1/2 t baking soda
1/2 t salt
2 t caraway seeds
1 egg
1/4 c olive oil
1/3 c water

Olive oil, for cooking

PROCESS:
Whisk together first five ingredients in a small mixing bowl.

In another bowl whisk together egg, oil, and water.

Add liquid to dry mixture and stir well.

Pre-heat small skillet (about 6 inches) with 1 t of oil and pour in 1/2 c of the batter.

Shuffle skillet gently to ensure batter is distributed evenly.

Cook for 5 minutes per side over a medium-low heat, or until the exterior is crisp and golden.

Repeat and enjoy!

Notes: The focaccia-like texture of this bread works well with Italian seasoning. Substitute Italian seasoning for caraway seeds for a new twist.

About this Recipe
PALEO / DAIRY FREE / COCONUT FREE / VEGETARIAN / GLUTEN FREE

SANDWICH LOAF

There is nothing quite like the smell of a homemade yeast bread in the oven. For many of us who don't have gluten in our diets any longer this experience has been a thing of the past. Fret not, this bread will bring you right back to your pre-gluten free days and evoke smiles all around. While it's best enjoyed day one, you can refrigerate this bread and toast it for up to 3 days.

YIELD:

1 loaf (8.5" X 4.5" X 2.5" loaf pan)

INGREDIENTS:

1/2 c warm water

2 t active dry yeast

1 t of raw sugar

2 c + 2 - 5 T CSC gluten free flour (*pg 89*)

1 t salt

2 t xanthan gum

3/4 c + 1 T hot water

3 T olive oil

1 egg, beaten until frothy

PROCESS:

In a small bowl, sprinkle yeast evenly over water and sugar. Set aside and allow to grow for 15 minutes.

Meanwhile, combine dry ingredients with a whisk and set aside.

In a large bowl pour in hot water, then olive oil, then gradually temper in egg as to not cook.

Next, gently add yeast mixture and stir. Add flour in slowly, 1/2 c at a time, stirring gently as you go. Allow mixture to sit for 5 minutes to absorb moisture.

Then add another 2 - 5 T of flour, stirring, until a soft dough is formed.*

Stir vigorously (in place of kneading) for about 30 seconds.

Transfer dough to an oiled bowl and cover with a dish towel. Place the bowl in a warm place with no drafts.

Allow dough to rise for 1h 15m. Then "punch" dough and transfer to oiled loaf pan to rise for another hour. Bake at 400 degrees F for 30-35 minutes.

*Notes: A great place to proof bread dough is in your unheated oven. Just turn on the oven light to ensure the space stays warm. *Unlike a traditional bread dough, this dough cannot be shaped into a loaf. By omitting wheat flour and the gluten it contains, the dough ends up softer and less elastic. However, it still should be dense enough that it will transfer from the mixing bowl into the oiled bowl using a spoon and without leaving much, if any, dough behind.*

About this Recipe
DAIRY FREE / COCONUT FREE / NUT FREE / VEGETARIAN / GLUTEN FREE

Sweets & Treats

cleansoutherncuisine.com

AMARETTO POUND CAKE

A pound cake is a staple in the South. They've graced church potluck dinner tables, picnic tables, and even holiday tables. This unfussy dessert is great for a multitude of occasions, travels well, and the slices can even be enjoyed sans plate or fork. Perhaps that's why I have so many memories of eating it on family camping trips as a child.

YIELD:

1 standard pound cake

INGREDIENTS:

1 3/4 c almond flour

1 1/2 c tapioca flour

3/4 c arrowroot

1 t xanthan gum (optional)

1/3 c + 1 T amaretto

1/3 c full fat coconut milk

3/4 c coconut oil

1 t almond extract

2 t vanilla extract

1 t baking soda

2 t cream of tartar

1 t salt

3/4 c coconut sugar

4 eggs

PROCESS:

Preheat oven to 325 degrees F. Grease pan generously with coconut oil and set aside.

Whisk together first four ingredients (dry ingredients) and set aside.

Combine amaretto and coconut milk (wet ingredients) and set aside.

Add coconut oil, extracts, baking soda, cream of tartar, salt, and sugar to your stand mixer and beat until fluffy.

Add eggs, one at a time, allowing each to be fully beaten in before adding the next.

While beating at a low speed, alternate adding dry ingredients and wet ingredients that you previously set aside, starting and ending with the dry ingredients.

Beat until just combined taking care not to overbeat! Your batter will be very viscous and somewhat elastic.

Pour into bundt pan and bake for 45 - 55 minutes.

A toothpick inserted into the middle of the cake should come out almost clean. Remember that when using almond flour the toothpick will almost never be spotless.

Allow cake to cool in pan for 5-10 minutes then transfer to a wire rack to cool for another 30 minutes before serving.

Notes: Serve with fresh berries and coconut whipped cream if desired.

About this Recipe
PALEO / DAIRY FREE / VEGETARIAN / GLUTEN FREE

CRANBERRY COOKIES

Growing up, my sisters and I adored the children's book Cranberry Christmas. It included a recipe for cranberry cookies, which my family adapted to our liking over the years. Around Christmastime, we always looked forward to these unique cookies rather than the sea of overly saccharine ones. Fresh cranberries deliver a pleasant tartness, as well as antioxidants. I have overhauled the recipe and utilize almond flour for a more filling, high-protein treat.

YIELD:

30 cookies

INGREDIENTS:

Dry Ingredients:

2 cups superfine almond flour

1/2 c tapioca flour

1/2 c arrowroot powder

1 t baking powder

1/2 t baking soda

1/2 t salt

Other Ingredients:

1/2 c organic grassfed butter

1 c organic coconut sugar
or raw sugar

2 eggs

2 T lemon juice fresh squeezed

3 cups fresh cranberries,
chopped

2 cups walnuts, chopped

Zest of one small lemon
or 1/2 large lemon

PROCESS:

Preheat oven to 375 degrees F. Combine dry ingredients and set aside.

Cream butter and sugar in a large bowl until fluffy.

Slowly beat in eggs and lemon juice.

Add dry ingredients into wet ingredients about 1 cup at a time.

Stir in cranberries, lemon zest, and walnuts until just combined.

Refrigerate dough for an hour.

Using a scoop or spoons make 2T mounds of dough on a parchment lined baking sheet.

Give cookies space as they will spread.

Bake for 20 - 25 minutes, or until edges turn just golden.

Notes: This recipe is easiest made in a stand mixer. These tender cookies will not brown much.

About this Recipe
PALEO / DAIRY FREE / COCONUT FREE / VEGETARIAN / GLUTEN FREE

LEMON ICEBOX PIE

Sometimes life calls for a pie. Sometime allergies call for no eggs. We've got y'all covered! This gut-friendly rendition of a lemon pie uses gelatin instead of eggs. It's a refreshing treat any time of year but really shines in the warmer months or after a rich meal.

YIELD:

one 9" pie

INGREDIENTS:

3/4 c water

4 1/2 t beef gelatin

1 c lemon juice (5 - 6 lemons)

1 T lemon zest

3/4 c raw sugar or coconut sugar

1 can full fat coconut milk (13.5 oz)

1/2 t vanilla extract

Pie Crust
(pg 150 or 151)

PROCESS:

In a small bowl, sprinkle gelatin over water and allow to bloom for 5 minutes.

In a medium saucepan heat lemon juice and sugar until hot, not boiling. Turn off heat.

Add gelatin mixture to hot mixture and whisk for 2 minutes.

Add coconut milk, vanilla extract, and zest.

Chill for 30 minutes or until the filling has thickened slightly.

Pour into a prebaked pie crust and refrigerate for 4 more hours.

Notes: Serve with coconut whipped cream and fresh blueberries. Try Vital Proteins brand of unflavored and grass fed beef gelatin.

About this Recipe
PALEO / DAIRY FREE / EGG FREE / AIP / NUT FREE / VEGETARIAN / GLUTEN FREE

COCONUT BLENDER CUPCAKES

Similar to an Italian wedding cake if you choose to add the pecans, these delicately sweet cupcakes have layers of coconut flavor and go well with just about any topping or frosting. The best thing about them? You won't even dirty a mixing bowl... all of the ingredients go right into your high-powered blender. *pictured with chocolate ganache*

YIELD:

12 cupcakes

INGREDIENTS:

8 eggs

3/4 c palm shortening, melted

3 T full fat coconut milk

2 t coconut extract

2 t vanilla extract

1/2 t salt

1/2 c coconut sugar

3/4 c coconut flour

1 1/2 t baking powder

1 c unsweetened shredded coconut

1 c chopped pecans, toasted (optional)

PROCESS:

Preheat oven to 350 degrees F. Crack eggs into blender and blend on low speed for about 1 minute to incorporate air.

Add in coconut milk, palm shortening, extracts, and sugar. Blend for another minute.

Meanwhile mix together flour, salt, and baking powder. Stop blender and add the dry mixture.

Blend until just incorporated.
Batter will be significantly thicker.

Remove blender from base and fold in pecans and shredded coconut by hand.

Line a muffin pan with paper liners or coat each slot with a generous amount of palm shortening.

Pour batter into pan, filling each slot about 3/4 of the way full.

Bake for 15 - 18 minutes.

Cool and enjoy!

Notes: These cupcakes, like many coconut flour baked goods, will become much more moist the day after if stored in an airtight container. Store and enjoy for up to 4 days.

About this Recipe
PALEO / DAIRY FREE / AIP / VEGETARIAN / GLUTEN FREE

ORANGE SPONGE CAKE

When I think of sponge cake I think of my outspoken and beloved Granny saying "A sponge cake is just fine for diabetics." (Draw out the "fine") Bernice B. Gipson was herself a diabetic and obviously wanted to have her pleasures. Perhaps sponge cake was the best option in her heyday as it typically wasn't loaded with sugary frosting or icing. If she were still here today I would want to share this cake with her and tell her that this one, in moderation, would indeed be "just fiiiine" for diabetics as the fat from the almond flour tends to keep blood sugar levels from spiking so high. Here's to remembering you and all of your color, Granny. *Pictured with Orange Curd on Granny's cake stand*

YIELD:
2 - 8" round layers

INGREDIENTS:
Dry Ingredients:
2 c almond flour
1 c tapioca flour
1/2 c arrowroot powder
2 T coconut flour
2 1/2 t baking powder
1 T orange zest

Wet Ingredients Part 1:
3/4 c palm shortening
3/4 c raw sugar or coconut sugar
1 t orange extract
1 t vanilla extract
1 t salt
5 large eggs

Wet Ingredients Part 2:
1/4 c orange liqueur, like
Grand Marnier
1/2 c unsweetened almond milk

PROCESS:
Preheat oven to 350 degrees F. Combine dry ingredients in a medium bowl.

In a stand mixer beat palm shortening with sugar, extracts, and salt until fluffy. While this beats combine wet ingredients part 2.

Next, add eggs one at a time. Allow each egg yoke to disappear before adding the next.

Alternate adding Dry Ingredients and Wet Ingredients Part 2 mixture. Start and end with Dry Ingredients.

Transfer batter to generously greased 8" round pans.

Bake for 20 - 25 minutes. Allow cakes to cool in pans for 10 minutes prior to turning out on a cooling rack.

Notes: Serve this cake "naked", with whipped coconut cream, or with a luscious orange curd.

About this Recipe
PALEO / DAIRY FREE / VEGETARIAN / GLUTEN FREE

MINI BLUEBERRY SCONES

My oldest sister, Rebecca, is one of the most talented bakers I know despite the fact she has no formal training. The confections she can turn out of her kitchen could easily be featured on the shelves of any fabulous bakery in any prominent city. She is also a natural hostess and creates themed parties and events for lucky friends and family members to enjoy. I think these slightly sweet blueberry scones have a place at her next tea party or British Royals event.

YIELD:
16 small scones

INGREDIENTS:
2 1/2 c CSC Gluten Free Flour (*pg. 89*)

2 t baking powder

1/4 t baking soda

1/2 t salt

1/2 t xanthan gum

1/4 c coconut oil

1/4 c palm shortening

2 eggs

1/3 c unsweetened macadamia or almond milk

1 1/2 t vanilla

1/4 c agave

1 t lemon zest

1 1/2 c fresh whole blueberries

PROCESS:
Preheat oven to 375 degrees F. Place coconut oil and palm shortening in freezer to harden for 20 minutes.

Combine first five ingredients in a mixing bowl. Using a fork or pastry blender, cut the hardened oil mixture into the flour mixture.

Mix together wet ingredients and zest in a small bowl and then add them to dry ingredients, stirring until just combined.

Gently fold in blueberries.

Roll dough out onto a floured surface forming two rectangles (about 3" x 10") then cut each into 8 triangles using diagonal cuts.

Transfer to a parchment lined baking sheet and bake for 17 - 20 minutes.

Notes: Your dough may become fairly blue as the fresh blueberries are delicate. Not to worry as these scones are somewhat rustic and will taste delicious all the same!

About this Recipe
PALEO / DAIRY FREE / NUT FREE / VEGETARIAN / GLUTEN FREE

BOURBON BALLS

No powdered sugar or processed cookie ingredients here. You won't believe these ambrosial treats actually contain fiber and magnesium. Bourbon balls have long been a holiday favorite of the South. Be forewarned that you should always double the recipe if you are going to a larger social engagement... these tend to be show-stealers and folks will eat more than one. This recipe is for my girlfriend Kate - who hails from Kentucky - and who taught me to appreciate bourbon in multiple applications.

YIELD:
24 bourbon balls

INGREDIENTS:
1 1/4 c pecans, chopped
1/2 c bourbon
1/2 c ghee, melted
1/4 c maple syrup
1/4 c agave nectar
1/2 t vanilla
3 T coconut flour
1 T raw cacao powder
1 T arrowroot flour
1/8 t sea salt
1 c + 1/2 c non dairy
chocolate chips
2 T coconut oil

Whole pecans
for garnish
Coarse sea salt
for garnish

• *PHOTO ON
PAGE 133*

PROCESS:
Soak chopped pecans in bourbon overnight.
Add pecans, any excess bourbon, and 1/2 c chocolate chips to your food processor. Process to a very fine chop.

In a small bowl combine melted ghee, maple syrup, agave nectar, and vanilla.

Next whisk in coconut flour, raw cacao, arrowroot, and sea salt until mixture is smooth.

Working quickly add the liquid to the ingredients in your food processor and pulse until well combined.

Freeze mixture for 30 minutes.

Remove hardened bourbon ball mixture from freezer and shape into balls, about 1" circumference.

Melt 1 c chocolate chips. Stir in 2 T of coconut oil. If you are using a very dark chocolate you may need to add more coconut oil.

Drop balls one by one into the melted chocolate mixture. Coat well by using a spoon to swirl the chocolate around the ball.

Transfer balls to a parchment lined baking sheet and top with a whole pecan or coarse sea salt.

Refrigerate for at least 30 minutes to allow chocolate to harden.

Notes: Be sure to use a brand of bourbon that is gluten free. You can make this recipe by hand but a food processor will make your task a lot easier.

About this Recipe
PALEO / DAIRY FREE / EGG FREE / VEGETARIAN / GLUTEN FREE

I DREAM OF CHOCOLATE COOKIES

Y'all, I really do!…. Dream of chocolate and chocolate cookies that is. One of my favorite superfoods is raw cacao powder as an alternative to chocolate or standard cocoa powder (which has had most nutrients roasted out of it). Did you know that one serving of raw cacao contains more magnesium than a serving of spinach? If you are going to make cookies and consume some sort of sugar you might as well have added health benefits along with it!

YIELD:
2 dozen

INGREDIENTS:
1 1/2 c CSC Gluten Free Flour
(pg 89)
1 t baking powder
1/2 t baking soda
1/2 t salt
1 1/2 t xanthan gum

1/4 c coconut oil, melted
1/4 c palm shortening, melted
1/4 c maple syrup
1 1/2 t vanilla extract
2 eggs, beaten
1/3 c raw cacao powder
1/4 c coconut sugar

1/2 c chocolate chips
3/4 c toasted pecans, chopped

PROCESS:
Preheat oven to 350 degrees F. In a small bowl whisk the first five ingredients together and set aside.

In a medium bowl, whisk together the next five ingredients.

Add in raw cacao and coconut sugar, whisking once more until mixture is smooth.

Slowly incorporate the flour mixture into the liquid mixture, stirring as you go.

Last, stir in chocolate chips and pecans. Dough will be very thick.

Scoop rounded tablespoons of dough onto a parchment lined baking sheet and gently flatten and shape each cookie.

Bake for 10 - 14 minutes.

*Notes: *To make these cookies vegan just substitute 2 T flaxseed meal and 5 T of water for the eggs. You will need to combine these two ingredients and allow them to sit for five minutes. For fudgy cookie centers cook for only 10 minutes.*

About this Recipe
VEGAN* / DAIRY FREE / VEGETARIAN / GLUTEN FREE

BROWN BUTTER
CHOCOLATE PECAN COOKIES

Brown butter is just butter than has been gently boiled until the milk fat starts to brown. It results in a nutty, rich taste and an out of this universe aroma! When you pair brown butter with pecans, perhaps the south's most favored nut, you get something amazing. So for those of you who love a chocolate chip cookie with some flair, bring these to your next social engagement – they will definitely up your cookie game!

YIELD:
2 dozen

INGREDIENTS:
1 1/3 c cassava flour or 180 g

1/3 c pecans, finely chopped

1 1/2 t cream of tartar

3/4 t baking soda

1/2 t salt

1/4 c butter

1/4 c palm shortening

3/4 c toasted pecans, chopped

1/4 c coconut sugar

1/4 c maple syrup

1 1/2 t vanilla extract

2 eggs

1/2 c chocolate chips

PROCESS:
Preheat oven to 350 degrees F. Whisk first five ingredients together and set aside.

In a small saucepan melt butter and palm shortening. When it comes to a boil lower heat so that in continues to gently boil. Butter will start to turn darker in color, about 5 minutes. Stir in toasted chopped pecans and allow them to cook in the butter for 2 minutes.

Remove saucepan from heat to cool for 15 - 20 minutes.

Whisk sugar, maple syrup, vanilla extract, and eggs into the butter mixture.

Pour butter mixture into the dry ingredients and stir until well combined.

Last, stir in chocolate chips.

Scoop rounded tablespoons of dough onto parchment lined baking sheet and gently flatten and shape each cookie.

Bake for 10 - 12 minutes, until the bottoms are just brown.

Notes: I used Otto's brand cassava flour for this recipe. Other brands have not been tested.

About this Recipe
PALEO / VEGETARIAN / GLUTEN FREE

GLUTEN FREE PIE CRUST

Craving a perfectly buttery and flaky pie crust? You've found it! This crust uses my signature flour blend – CSC Gluten Free Flour – to achieve a traditional end result worthy of any filling. This recipe makes two crusts as I find freezing one for future use can be extremely helpful. You'll thank yourself later.

YIELD:
Makes TWO pie crusts

INGREDIENTS:
2 1/2 c CSC Gluten Free Flour *(pg 85)*

2 T coconut flour (powdered)

1 1/2 t xanthan gum

3/4 t salt

1 1/4 c butter

1/2 - 2/3 c cold water

PROCESS:
Preheat oven to 350 degrees F. Whisk or sift first four ingredients together.

Using a fork or pastry blender cut butter into flour mixture until you get pea-sized crumbles.

Then add ice cold water into the mixture gradually, stirring until the dough just comes together. Do not add any more water beyond this point.

Cut into two equal portions and roll out on a generously floured surface.

The crust should be about 12" in diameter if you are using a standard 9" pie pan. Once the desired thickness is reached, carefully transfer it to a lightly oiled pie pan and shape the edges as desired.

Transfer to an oiled pie pan and shape edges.

Prick bottom of crust several times with a fork.

Bake for 25 - 30 minutes, or until pie crust is golden in color. Allow to cool completely before adding filling.

*Notes: *To make this recipe dairy free/vegan use palm shortening. Be sure to freeze it first and work quickly as it melts more rapidly than butter.*

About this Recipe
VEGAN / PALEO / DAIRY FREE* / EGG FREE / COCONUT FREE / NUT FREE / VEGETARIAN / GLUTEN FREE*

PALEO PIE CRUST

A pie crust is not something that you think of as a low maintenance recipe. However, this press-in pie crust is a breeze to pull together. No blending of butter and no rolling of dough really cuts down on the time. This crust works well with both savory and sweet fillings.

YIELD:

1 pie crust suitable for
a 9" pie pan

INGREDIENTS:

1 c almond flour

1 c tapioca flour

1/3 c arrowroot

1/2 t sea salt

1/4 c coconut oil, melted

1/4 c warm water

PROCESS:

Preheat oven to 350 degrees F. Lightly grease pie pan with coconut oil and set aside.

Whisk together dry ingredients in a bowl.

Melt coconut oil and stir into dry ingredients.

Next add warm water until you reach desired consistency. You may need to add an extra 1 - 2 T or possibly more.

Form dough into a ball and then flatten and press into a greased 9" pie pan.

Bake at 350 for 30 - 35 minutes. Allow crust to cool completely prior to filling it.

Notes: This crust will not brown much. If you can tolerate butter use it in place of the coconut oil as the milk solids will cause the crust to brown.

About this Recipe
VEGAN / PALEO / DAIRY FREE / EGG FREE / VEGETARIAN / GLUTEN FREE

Drinks & Juices

cleansoutherncuisine.com

BEGINNERS BLENDER JUICE

New to green juices? This approachable juice will help you to ease your way in. As you become accustomed to the flavors of vegetable juices you can decrease the fruit, increase the vegetables, and add a cup of leafy greens to the mix. Just toss all ingredients into a high powered blender and voila!

YIELD:

1 serving

INGREDIENTS:

1 green apple, quartered

1/2 c cantaloupe or other melon

1 stalk of celery,
cut into 3" pieces

1/2 c cucumber

1 t lime juice

3/4 c chilled coconut water

1 c baby spinach, optional

PROCESS:

Add all ingredients to the blender.

Blend, increasing speed to high, for 1 minute or until juice is completely smooth.

Notes: All juices are best consumed immediately. Not only do they taste better but you get the most benefit from immediate consumption. Once oxidation begins the natural enzymes in fruits and veggies begin to break down.

• *PHOTO ON PAGE 153*

About this Recipe
VEGAN / PALEO / DAIRY FREE / EGG FREE / AIP / COCONUT FREE / NUT FREE / VEGETARIAN / GLUTEN FREE*

COLLAGEN HOT CHOCOLATE

Sometimes life calls for a hot chocolate. It feels extremely indulgent to have this for breakfast yet its ingredients pack a nutritional punch. By trading traditional cocoa powder for a raw cacao powder you get tons of magnesium, flavonols, and antioxidants. You can spike this hot chocolate and add a touch of cinnamon for holiday entertaining.

YIELD:

1 serving

INGREDIENTS:

1 1/2 c non dairy milk

1 T raw agave

1 T raw cacao

1/8 t vanilla

2 scoops (about 20 g) collagen peptides or hydrolyzed collagen

PROCESS:

In a small saucepan, heat milk over medium heat. Remove from heat once milk is smoking (just before boiling).

Add agave, vanilla, and cocoa powder. Whisk thoroughly.

Last, add in collagen peptides and whisk until dissolved.

Transfer to mug and enjoy!

*Notes: This recipe works well with almond milk. For a richer drink use 3/4 c full fat coconut milk and 3/4 c water. *Using coconut milk will also make this recipe Vegan, AIP, and Nut Free. *Using stevia in place of agave will make this recipe Ketogenic.*

About this Recipe
VEGAN / PALEO / DAIRY FREE / EGG FREE / AIP* / KETOGENIC* / COCONUT FREE / NUT FREE* / VEGETARIAN / GLUTEN FREE*

PINEAPPLE PEPPER GREEN JUICE

This lively juice doesn't require a fancy juicer. Just blend well in your high powered blender and you'll be sipping or slurping in no time. If you are new to green juices try Beginners Blender Juice (pg 154) first.

YIELD:

1 serving

INGREDIENTS:

1 c coconut water or water

2 t fresh lemon juice

1/4" cube ginger

1 c kale,
destemmed and packed

1 c frozen pineapple chunks

Pinch of cayenne pepper,
optional

PROCESS:

Thoroughly wash all produce.

Place ingredients in blender in the order listed above.

Blend on high until all bits of kale disappear.

Enjoy immediately!

*Notes: Be sure to remove any kale stems before juicing. Any type of kale will work well in this juice. Lacitano kale is time saver as you can typically just rip the leaves right off of the stems with very little effort. No cutting board and knife required! *To make this juice AIP simply omit the cayenne pepper.*

About this Recipe
VEGAN / PALEO / DAIRY FREE / EGG FREE / AIP / COCONUT FREE / NUT FREE / VEGETARIAN / GLUTEN FREE*

TART CHERRY ROYALE

Tart cherry juice may be antioxidant-rich and boast lots of health benefits but it's also delicious. Having always been a fan of sparkling wine and champagne, I love a bubbly-based drink. This one is simple and pretty in a champagne flute. What's better than bubbles with benefits?

YIELD:

2 servings y'all!

INGREDIENTS:

4 oz prosecco

1 oz tart cherry juice

1 pitted cherry, for garnish

1 oz satsuma or orange juice, optional

Splash of orange liqueur, optional

PROCESS:

Pour prosecco into champagne flute.

Follow with all other ingredients and give it a stir.

Drop a cherry into the glass and garnish the rim with a satsuma slice.

About this Recipe
PALEO / DAIRY FREE / EGG FREE / COCONUT FREE / NUT FREE / VEGETARIAN / GLUTEN FREE

CHOCOLATE (NUT) MILK

When I was a kid creamy chocolate milk was a favorite treat of mine. This milk is reminiscent of traditional chocolate milk when you add the optional agave. However, unlike its traditional counterpart, it's loaded with potassium, magnesium, and protein thanks to its power-packed ingredients.

YIELD:
2 1/2 cups (2 servings)

INGREDIENTS:
1/2 c soaked cashews

2 1/4 c cold coconut water

1 T raw cacao powder

1 t agave, optional

PROCESS:
Cover cashews in water and soak for 4 hours or up to overnight.

Drain cashews.

Place all ingredients in high powered blender and blend on high speed for one minute.

Enjoy!

Notes: Add collagen peptides to this milk to up the protein content and nutritional benefit. You can make ahead and store this milk in your refrigerator for up to 3 days.

About this Recipe
VEGAN / PALEO / DAIRY FREE / EGG FREE / VEGETARIAN / GLUTEN FREE

ACKNOWLEDGMENTS AND THANKS

To Izabella, for listening to me go on and on about entertaining and Southern food and subsequently pointing out that I should really just write a cookbook. Your mission and drive to help so many reclaim their health has been a huge inspiration to me. Thanks to you and Michael for your guidance and support!

To my Mama, Louann, who taught me to cook and to not be afraid of seasoning! Thank you for teaching me manners, to look on the bright side, and to punctuate with the word "honey". You are a true lady and I'm so lucky to call you Mom.

To my Daddy, Doug, for teaching me to say "Howdy, Boo, and Bye" to everyone I meet…which led me to a career in hospitality and a new level of culinary education. Also for teaching me about mechanics, plumbing, roofing, and all manner of other things little girls should know about. It's all come in handy more than once - especially the expert parallel parking skills.

To my sisters Rebecca and Jennifer for being the best two older sisters a girl could ask for. I don't think my feet touched the ground the first two years of my life but once I was semi-independent of your hips you began to encourage me to spread my wings and experience art, culture, music, and explore places other than where we grew up. These things informed the lens through which I view the world and I am eternally grateful. If it weren't for you I may not have ever fully appreciated the culinary riches of our youth.

To Laura, my oldest friend, for many adventures and many to come… and for being my "Cajun lifeline" and confidant when I needed a second opinion, feedback, or inspiration for this book.

To Fallon, for listening to me drone on about this project for what feels like forever now and for encouraging me to keep going through the toughest times.

To my Robert - your support has been unwavering through these past few years. Thank you for teaching me photography. Your ability to teach yourself and master almost anything is pretty darn cool. While many think that your role through this all has been feasting on a constant parade of delicacies, few have seen "behind the curtains". Thank you for dealing with unending loads of dishes so I could continue recipe testing, thank you for your honesty when things tasted sub-par, thank you for the many nights and weekends you made it a point not to distract me from my project, and also for recognizing when I needed a break. Thank you for your vision, encouragement, and praise, but most of all thank you for making me cackle. Laughing is one thing, but being driven to belly laugh and cackle on a near daily basis is entirely another…and for that I am truly grateful.

You might be wondering why the peacock? Simply put, I've always had an affinity for peacocks. Their vibrant colors and huge spray of tail feathers are one of those things that just make me marvel at the artistry of nature. They are also fairly prevalent where I grew up and I think one of the most gorgeous scenes is a peacock near a sprawling live oak tree draped in Spanish Moss.

Index | By Chapter and Recipe Title

Additional Acknowledgements

~~Page 63~~
At the time this book was published, Emeril's Sweet Potato and Andouille Soup recipe was no longer available online. You can find other recipes by Emeril Lagasse at www.emerils.com.

Page 137
Delvin, W. (1976). Cranberry Christmas, New York: Four Winds Press
Visit harryandwendedevlin.com for more info.

Cookbook Design / Production / Illustrations by Kate Ferry / kateferry33@mac.com

Made in the USA
Coppell, TX
25 June 2020